LIVING THE LOVE OF GOD

By the Same Author

LIVING THE LOVE
OF GOD

Reflections upon the Knowledge and Love of God

By

CARROLL E. SIMCOX
Editor, *The Living Church*

MOREHOUSE-BARLOW CO.
NEW YORK

© 1965 by Morehouse-Barlow Co.

Library of Congress Catalog Card No. 65-27002

159567

241
Sᴧ62

PRINTED IN THE UNITED STATES OF AMERICA

To Henry I. Louttit:

friend, bishop
and man of God

Contents

LIVING THE LOVE OF GOD

CHAPTER I

Prebeginnings

ANYBODY WHO HAS given any thought at all to the meaning of such terms as "knowing" and "loving" God has soon come to see that one cannot know or love God in the way that one knows or loves any other being. I can love my spouse, or mother, or son, or even my enemy, for certain good or at least understandable reasons—so long as he or she is human like me. But my beloved must be human, or perhaps subhuman. I can love my dog; but, if I do, it will be for those "almost human" things I see, or imagine I see, in him. What is inconceivable is that my beloved should be suprahuman and yet lovable to me. God is supra-human. He has nothing in common with me.* How on earth then, or how in heaven, can I reasonably be re-quired to love Him?

When we consider how we come to know and to love a human person, we find that several factors usually enter in.†

It is virtually necessary to be physically where the

---

* God becomes man, takes our humanity upon Himself, in the Incarnation. But He remains divine, infinitely suprahuman, in His own being. So if He is to be loved it must be as God.

† Throughout this book I speak of knowing and loving God as a single act. One must know Him to love Him, one must love Him to know Him.

other person is, in direct contact. Most human loves begin, at least, in such face-to-face meeting. It would be hard for most of us to fall in love with somebody purely by correspondence.

This person-to-person meeting, if it is to become a union of love, must have at its heart some common, shared experience which fosters an intimate closeness between the persons. Social or personal equality is not required. In a rigid caste system there can be, and often is, true love between persons of widely differing stations. What is required, normally, is that their love be rooted in some human solidarity—a common grief, joke, fear, hobby, any of a thousand possible human experiences, enthusiasms, and enterprises.

You find that it helps you immensely to love another person if that person is easily likable and attractive to you. It seems to me that too many of our young clergy fresh from seminary feel that they have not reached their homiletical majority until they have preached that pulpit-shocker on how a Christian can love somebody while heartily disliking him. Some of these sermons seem almost to make a Christian virtue out of detesting the person whom one is "loving" for Christ's sake. This of course is never the preacher's intent. What he's trying to drive home is the very important truth that Christian loving, which is an act of the will in obedience of the mind of Christ, must be distinguished from all forms of emotional, esthetic, or erotic attachment to the beloved. True though this is, it doesn't alter the fact that if you can heartily like somebody you find it easier to love him.

If your beloved has done something nice for you, this helps your loving. And by one of the bright paradoxes of love, if you do something nice for him it may help your loving even more.

Your friend's very faults can endear him to you, evidently because he and you are united in the common experience of being sinners. Yes, you say, I know he drinks too much, and in him the threshold between fact and fancy is rather low, and he's vain as a popinjay; but he's human, bless him, and so am I!

In some such ways, you can come to love another human being and to grow in your love of him. But not God. It would be lunacy for any man to talk about sharing experiences with the Almighty, or to say of Him, "He's human, bless Him, and so am I!" There is no common essence or sharable experience which can provide a basis for comradeship between God and man.* We wish there were. We wish God were human. Herod, in W. H. Auden's *For the Time Being*, speaks of the kind of prayer which his subjects are constantly sending up:

> O God, put away justice and truth for we cannot understand them and do not want them. Eternity would bore us dreadfully. Leave Thy heavens and come down to our earth of waterclocks and hedges. Become our uncle. Look after Baby, amuse Grandfather, escort Madam to the Opera, help Willy with his home-work, introduce Muriel to a handsome naval officer. Be interesting and weak like us, and we will love you as we love ourselves.[1]

---

* Although I did once know a pious gentleman of the now defunct early-twentieth-century-liberal-Protestant school who wrote a book entitled *Finding the Comrade God*. Whether theology as a whole is in better shape today than it was forty years ago when my friend was finding the Comrade God, only God knows; but I cannot but think that it is gain that there is less of this chumminess with deity than there was then.

Of course we should; but God refuses to be interesting, weak, and "like us."

I am simply stating this problem, not creating it. We are commanded to love God; but to love Him for the reasons we have for loving a human being is impossible because He is not human. This problem gets astonishingly little attention from Christian thinkers today.*

Christians say that the knowledge and love of God is man's chief end, his reason for being, his *summum bonum*. In the New Testament it is called our eternal life: "And this is life eternal, that they might know thee the only true God, and Jesus Christ, whom thou hast sent" (St. John 17:3). According to the New Testament, if we do not know and love God we are worse off than dead. Christ came, died, and rose again to give us this knowledge and love of God which is our eternal life. It is incontestably the most important thing in life, if Christianity is to be believed. But suppose we believe this; how do we go about entering this lifegiving knowledge and love?

Jean Pierre Camus, Bishop of Belley, was the Boswell of St. Francis de Sales (1567-1622). He once asked Francis how one can best become perfect. The Saint answered, "You must love God with your whole heart, and

---

* I am not forgetting the several major opera on the nature of love by such eminent thinkers as Anders Nygren (Lutheran), C. S. Lewis (Anglican), and M. C. d'Arcy, S.J. (Roman Catholic). But these are studies of love in its various forms: *agape* (self-giving love), *eros* (desire), *philia* (friendship), etc. It is not the purpose of any of these writers to show you how you can know and love God. They leave this counsel to others, and they have every right to do so; but I am astonished that so few Christians writers take up the task.

your neighbor as yourself." How else, indeed, could a Christian saint answer this question? His friend then asked him *how* one can so love, and Francis replied, again with the inevitable and only possible answer for a very advanced saint: "The best way, the shortest and easiest way of loving God with one's whole heart—is simply to love Him wholly and heartily! You learn to speak by speaking, to study by studying, to run by running, to work by working. Just so you learn to love God and man by loving. All those who wish to learn in any other way deceive themselves."[2]

This is perfect counsel—for some people; specifically, for those who are ready to receive it and to act upon it. The Saint might have mentioned also that a child learns to walk by walking. But before the child can begin this learning to walk by walking there must be certain indispensable developments in him. His muscles must be ready for the venture, and his mind must have developed to the point where he can watch his elders walking and decide that he would like very much to be able to get around as they do. Until these developments have occurred, there is no point in saying to the child, "You learn to walk by walking." For he is only a prebeginner, not yet ready to begin, not yet capable of beginning.

In the spiritual life, everybody must go through the stage of prebeginning. A person is ready to enter, and to begin growing in, the knowledge and love of God (which is the spiritual life, the eternal life) only when he has reached a position where he sees certain truths of his condition. He is ready to become a beginner when he sees his inability to handle his own life in his own way and on his own resources; the inability of his dearest human friends and lovers to do for him those things that most need to be done; his need for help and love from beyond and above himself; the love and power of God as revealed in Jesus Christ; and God's will to adopt him as His own child and eternal heir, to recreate him in the likeness of Christ by the power of the Holy Spirit.

I would not insist that a person must see these truths about God and himself in exactly the form in which I have just expressed them, but he must see essentially what St. Paul sees—that our sufficiency is of God and not of ourselves (II Corinthians 3:5). Moreover, he must see this not simply as a sound theological proposition to which he can subscribe intellectually, he must see and embrace it passionately with his whole being. Then, and only then, is he ready to enter the new life.

We must all start as prebeginners, which is what Christ means by saying that we must be born again. In America today are millions of prebeginners, many of them highly educated, morally mature, admired and admirable people. They may belong to churches, and yet be prebeginners. St. Francis de Sales' counsel about growing in the love of God by loving Him more might just as well be addressed to them in Old Norse. If they were entirely candid they would have to reply: How can we love Him whom we have not seen, with whom we have nothing human in common?

The people who came to St. Francis de Sales for counsel were not prebeginners but souls well established in the spiritual life. To be sure, that world probably had as high a percentage of prebeginners as ours has; but they were not the kind who came to Francis. If they had, I cannot imagine him advising them as he did his friend Camus, who was, after all, a quite advanced Christian.

Whatever was the situation then, it seems clear that we in our day cannot begin to consider the knowledge and love of God until we have made some sense of the pre-beginnings, the preparatory experiences, which are—I believe, as a Christian—God's "preparation of the Gospel" in the individual soul.

CHAPTER II

Preparation

ONE BECOMES A CHRISTIAN, is made the child of God, a member of Christ, and an heir of the kingdom of heaven, in Holy Baptism, and he may be baptized at the moment he is born. This the Church teaches, this most Christians believe, and this I believe. I make this public confession of faith now, so that what follows will be less likely to be misunderstood.

Certain things, which we are calling prebeginnings, must take place in a person before he can enter that new life which is the knowledge and love of God; and these things are present in the infant only in germ, as potentialities. The baptism of a child is an act of initiation into the new life in Christ, but it is also an act of anticipation. It is one thing to say of the infant who has just been baptized, "Now he is God's own child forever, by God's adoption and grace." It would be quite another thing to say of him, "He may not realize it himself, but already he knows and loves God, since he has been baptized into that supernatural experience of knowing and loving." To say this would be to take a desperate liberty with the plain meaning of plain words. The child of a day knows nothing and loves nobody, in the primary senses of those verbs.

The baptized infant is a child of God who begins his

filial life in total ignorance of his Father. God knows and loves him; and Holy Baptism, which should be seen as a divine act, is the pledge and seal of God's loving adoption of the child. But the child's response—his knowledge and love of God—is not yet. This child, if brought up in a devoutly Christian home and in the Church, may grow up into the knowledge and love of God by what is, to all appearances, a quiet, ordered, serene interior growth in grace, of the kind that William James had in mind when he spoke of "once-born" souls. He has begun his life under advantageous circumstances, and because of this his journey through the prebeginnings may be easier, pleasanter, with less travail in it. But in him, no less than in the person who has none of these initial advantages, there must be a preparatory experience of these prebeginnings if he is to be born again into the knowledge and love of God.

While I am trying to protect myself against certain misunderstandings I must say a word about semantics. These prebeginnings I shall be identifying by such labels as: instinct to suck, desire to be loved, desire to love, disillusionment with human love received, discovery of one's own insufficiency, longing for completeness and maturity as a person, realization of need for help and love from beyond and above one's self. These things could be called by other possibly better labels; I seek no quarrel about words. Then, some of my theories about how some of these things get started in a human life are simply and only this—my theories. For example, I may be wrong in thinking that the desire to be loved is essentially an outgrowth of the instinct to suck. But my, or anyone's, theory about the causation and filiation of such a thing is not essential to my argument itself—which is that these pre-beginnings can be a "preparation of the Gospel"* in our lives.

We begin our life, apparently, with no knowledge and love of God or even of ourselves; with only an instinct to suck. It may be hard to realize that there was a time in the life of Socrates, or Julius Caesar, or Moses, or Shake-speare, or Jesus, when there was this instinct to suck—and, so far as we know, nothing else. If this is correct, it seems that you and I begin our earthly race from the same starting-block as do these great ones. We start, as they did, with the instinct to suck.

As this instinct to suck is gratified, the infant lives and grows. And an awareness which he will never outgrow is being profoundly planted in the subconscious depth of his soul: the awareness that he began life as a total depend-

---

* The idea of a providential "preparation of the Gospel" dates back at least as far as St. Clement of Alexandria (c. A.D. 150-215) who said that "God is the source of all good things" and then proceeded to trace the consequences of this in human history. Greek philosophy was not a thing of the Devil simply because it was pagan. Rather it was given by God Himself to the Greeks "until the Lord should call the Greeks. For philosophy was a 'schoolmaster' to bring the Greek mind to Christ, as the Law brought the Hebrews. Thus philosophy was a preparation, paving the way towards perfection in Christ." (Clem. Alex. *Miscellanies*. I.v.28.) Christians since then have seen Greek philosophy, Roman order, Hebrew morality, and other such pre-Christian things as divinely ordered developments which God used to set the world stage for the saving gift of Christ. I think it equally proper to speak of a divinely ordered preparation of the Gospel in the individual soul, the ingredients of which are these prebeginnings we are thinking about.

ent upon the love of another person, which love came to him as milk. This is the first lesson to be learned by the growing soul.

Some months later, the instinct to suck begins to show itself as a desire to be loved. The child wants love in such tangible forms as food, toys, and personal attention. With him it is all getting, no giving. Waste no sermons to him on the text that it is more blessed to give than to receive; he's a long way short of that, and he may never get up to it at all. At the age of three, even the holiest saint was a pure and shameless getter, not a giver. We expect this in a small child, but if we find it in an adult we condemn it as infantile. We assume that a person in growing up must acquire a taste and a capacity for giving love as well as for receiving it; with us this is as axiomatic as that a civilized person eats from a plate rather than from a trough. The truly grown-up person does some active loving of his own; by this sign he is known as a grown-up person. In sum: *maturity in personality is maturity in the capacity to give love.*

The desire to be loved and the desire to love are two very distinct things which must not be confused. The former precedes the latter as its precondition; we can hardly imagine anybody growing up to the desire to love without having first experienced the more primitive desire to be loved.

The desire to be loved is, or at least can be, an outgrowth of the instinct to suck, and it may be regarded as a sign of conscious dependency upon love from outside one's self as necessary to life, no less than was milk at life's outset.

From this we turn to the desire to love, and we ask how this gets started in a human being. I suggest that we can see the birth of this desire to love and of active loving in a child, if we watch him carefully; and we shall see him learning to love by mimicry of his elders. The three-year-old "loves" his teddy bear by imitating his mother's loving him. He hugs and kisses it, calls it endearing names, because this—as he sees it—is the way that adults love. They are as gods to him, and "loving"—that is, hugs, caresses, smiles, and honey talk—is the most godlike thing they do. To be like them he must do as they do, and above all love as they love. He starts with his teddy bear. His clumsy mimicry is the birth of active (acting) love. If his parents believe that love is the greatest of all virtues they will encourage him in it, and, if they are sensible, they will let him go on "loving" his teddy bear without correction, since he is making a good start.

This seems to me to be the way a person normally learns to love, if he learns as a small child. Not all of us do. Any person *can* learn to love while still in the nursery, but it is by no means certain that he will. Love is always a decision, a choice, of the whole being. The desire to be loved may be purely involuntary and instinctive, as natural as sexual desire, but this is not true of the desire to love. At the risk of oversimplifying and overdogmatizing I will state my conviction, which is that the desire to love is born of the desire to mature, to grow up. The child "loving" his teddy bear associates loving with adulthood. The person of thirty or sixty who chooses to love, wills to love, does so because loving is escape from immaturity into maturity, as he sees it. If ever he becomes a totally committed Christian he will try to love as Christ loves because Christlikeness is his idea and ideal of perfect manhood, of full personal maturity.

And what of love for God? This too is something with which we are not born. One must learn to love God from others, and he must learn God's love for him through others. This should be no surprise or problem to Christians, since the central mystery of their redemption is Christ's mediation to them of the knowledge and love of God. "No man hath seen God at any time; the only begotten Son, which is in the bosom of the Father, he hath declared him" (St. John 1:18). To know Christ is to know God's love for us; yet we cannot know Christ except through the mediation of others. If this statement seems to call for some testing, we may imagine a child who has been given very little love by his parents, who reads the Gospels and learns God's love for him. He doesn't do this seeking and finding all by himself. There are four men, namely Sts. Matthew, Mark, Luke, and John, who bring to him the knowledge of God in Christ. No man finds his own way to God; every man must be brought by another. This most important truth should be fixed in mind: *We come to know God's loving concern for us through, and only through, the imperfect and faulty loving concern of some people for us.*

The time must come, however, when the child discovers the imperfection, faultiness, and insufficiency of the human love he receives and which he has hitherto considered his very life line. He may still be very young when he learns two harsh facts about his parents' love for him. One of these is that their love has in it some gaping holes and ugly flaws; the other is that it is mortal. Though they be the best of parents, the day comes when their love loses its salt, or its saltlessness stands nakedly revealed for the first time. They lie to him and get caught out, or they lose their tempers with him and he sees through it. Something or another happens which opens his eyes to the faultiness of their love. This is one disillusioning revelation. The other comes when he becomes fully conscious of death and its meaning. The appalling truth now bursts upon him that one day his parents will die—and with them their love for him. If he must live by their love, what then will become of him?

One of the Hebrew Psalmists went through this disillusionment with human and parental love, but later he could testify: "When my father and my mother forsake me, then the Lord will take me up" (Psalm 27:10). This is the classic pattern in the lives of the saints. The great knowers and lovers of God have used these disappointments and disillusionments with human love received as rungs on their ladders to heaven. Their experience has not made them cynical or misanthropic toward their fellows who love so imperfectly and mortally. It has only made them realize that, if they must live by love received, this love must be purer and stronger than any that man can give. Above all, it must be an immortal love which cannot die with the lover. He who comes to the vision of this truth is driven to it by what Vergil calls the Tears of Things.

So: the first great lesson the soul learns is that we live by the love of others—that we are loved into life and sustained in being by this love of others for us. Then follows the next great lesson, a hard one—that the love of other people for us is not enough. Some people, having learned this lesson, stop here. They console themselves as best they can with the philosophy which says, "Life was pleasanter in the nursery; but this world turns out to be not a nursery. Here we've got to stand on our own feet as best we can, taking things as they come and hoping for the best."

Some stop here. Others go on, to the knowledge and love of God.

CHAPTER III

"Givens"

ONE OF THE MOST influential of my literary spiritual guides is Baron Friedrich von Hügel. Almost everything he ever wrote seems to speak helpfully to my condition. This is true of a passage I shall quote now—but which cries for some supplementary comment. He writes:

> How much you can learn, as I myself have learnt, from watching cattle dreamily grazing and ruminating in their pastures! See how the sagacious creatures, without any theory or inflation of mind, instinctively select the herbs and grasses that suit and sustain them; and how they peacefully pass by what does not help them! They do not waste their time and energy in tossing away, or in trampling upon, or even simply in sniffing at, what is antipathetic to them. Why should they? Thistles may not suit *them;* well, there are other creatures in the world whom thistles *do* suit. And, in any case, are they the police of this rich and varied universe?"[1]

This is wise and pleasant counsel, but within some limits and with some qualifications. All that these cattle have to do to achieve their bovine beatitude is to take what they like and leave what they don't like among the various herbs in their pasture. Insofar as we have freedom to take what helps us and to leave what doesn't help us from among the sweet and bitter herbs in this world, we do well to imitate the cattle. But von Hügel would surely be the first to say that we have only some such freedom to choose. The cow doesn't have to swallow the thistle. Sometimes we do. As human beings we have to learn, as early as we can and as thoroughly as we can, how to live with, and to profit from, two distinct kinds of experience: the active and the passive, the things we choose to do and the things that are done to us whether we choose them or not.

There are these two kinds of experience in the lives of all of us—the things we do, and the things we suffer. No man, no matter how clever, resourceful, or lucky, is able so to rig life in his own favor that the things he does outweigh and outnumber the things he suffers. Freedom is the ability to *do*, and it is also the state of being unencumbered by the things done to us, by the "given" facts and factors of life from which there is no escape. On this definition, no man is entirely free. There is the freedom to choose and to do, and there is the necessity to endure the things done to us. And it appears plain, upon any searching, steady, and comprehensive inspection of human life, that the soul is affected by its handling of the things it suffers at least as vitally, if not more so, as it is by its handling of the things it does.

In the oldest and most human of our epics, Achilles is the mighty victor and Hector the valiant loser, which is another way of saying that Achilles *does* greatly while Hector *suffers* greatly. One might expect a supposedly "success-minded" race to make Achilles its hero in preference to Hector. But from the days of Homer onward the universal hero has been Hector, not Achilles. Nothing succeeds, it would seem, like a certain kind of failure.

This is no mere literary curiosity, but a disclosure, an *Offenbarung*, of the human race's deep awareness that man is revealed in how he suffers more than in what he does. Man is tested, and he is made or broken, in this crucible of passive experience of things done to him, things beyond his control, things that must be accepted and suffered.

Childhood for most of us, possibly for all of us, is pre-eminently the epoch of failure, of defeat. The adult who chatters about the carefree days of childhood might as well never have been a child; he has forgotten all. At every turn the child confronts pitiless reminders of his weakness, ignorance, and inadequacy. To be a child is to be—a person for whom the world is too much. Most parents do their best to shield, insulate, and narcotize the child against this dreadful reality, but this pretense can be kept up only for a while. If the child reaches adulthood without having learned that the world of "given" things is far too much for him, and that he cannot begin to cope with life on his own resources alone, he has been most expertly protected, or he is an idiot. In either case, he is wholly out of touch with reality.

During the transition period between childhood and adulthood some people suffer a delusion that they can handle life as it comes, with no help from outside themselves. In anybody of ordinary intelligence this delusion is only temporary. The fully mature person has come to realize that the dependency which characterized his childhood was not one of those childish things he can put away, but permanent. As a child he dreamt of that great day coming when he would be free: on his twenty-first birthday, perhaps; but upon becoming a man he learned that he would never be completely free in this life: free, that is, to be always a doer and never a sufferer, free from all necessity of accepting the things done to him.

What are the most important and influential things done to us, the "given" factors in life which affect most of us most? Sex, race, time in history, where we live, family, health, our opportunities and handicaps, our capacities and incapacities—these come readily to mind, and are enough to illustrate our point, which is this: that these "given" things may or may not be what we want, but we cannot change them, and our fate depends very largely upon how we live with them. Not on what they do to us, but how we live with them: this distinction is all-important. And obviously not all of these "given" factors are bad, in anybody's life, but some are likely to be. Here is a person whose IQ is above that of the moron but below what one really needs to hold his own in our world. It may be that before he dies some way will be found scientifically to correct such a deficiency in innate reasoning power. Meanwhile, this person must live out his days under the handicap of this harsh "given." He cannot be a genius. He can be a parasite, and miserable, or he can be a saint, and joyful. What he cannot be is a person free from this handicap.

Alcoholics Anonymous use a prayer which runs: "O God, give us the courage to change the things that can be changed, and the grace to accept the things that cannot be changed, and the wisdom to know the one from the other." There is no wisdom we need more than that.

When we reflect upon the harsher, crueler "givens"

which the soul can only suffer, and we bring God into our reflection, our usual course is to make a kind of scandal out of it. If God is good, and all-wise, and all-powerful, we ask, why does He give us these "givens", or let them happen to us, or whatever it is that He does or fails to do? This is an utterly futile line of questioning, of course. It leads nowhere. But "the grace to accept the things that cannot be changed" can be, for the suffering soul, the beginning of a life of intimate loving communion with God so glorious and rewarding in itself that the soul will end by thanking God for the burdens, limitations, and weaknesses which drove it to Him.

In *The Divine Milieu*, Pierre Teilhard de Chardin expresses with beautiful clarity what has always been the belief of Christ's faithful ones, in these words:

> In virtue of His very perfections, God cannot ordain that the elements of a world in the course of growth—or at least of a fallen world in the process of rising again—should avoid shocks and diminishments, even moral ones: *necessarium est ut scandala eveniant*.* But God will make it good—He will take His revenge, if one may use the expression—by making evil itself serve the higher good of His faithful, the very evil which the present state of creation does not allow Him to suppress immediately. Like an artist making use of a fault or an impurity in the stone he is sculpting or the bronze he is casting so as to produce more exquisite lines or a more beautiful tone, God, without sparing us the partial deaths, nor the final death, which form an essential part of our lives, transfigures them by integrating them in a better plan—*provided we trust lovingly in Him*. Not only our unavoidable ills but our faults, even our most deliberate ones, can be embraced in that transformation, provided always we repent of them. Not

* "It is necessary that offenses should come."

everything is immediately good to those who seek God; but everything is capable of becoming good: *omnia convertuntur in bonum*.[2]

I would fix attention upon the closing sentence—a great summing up indeed: "Not everything is immediately good to those who seek God; but everything is capable of becoming good." De Chardin has in mind Romans 8:28, well translated in the Revised Standard Version as: "We know that in everything God works for good with those who love him, who are called according to his purpose." A while ago I found myself citing, as an example of the kind of "given" which must be accepted and endured, the "given" of a dull, inadequate mind. One man who had to go through life with this handicap was a Frenchman named Jean Marie Baptiste Vianney (1786-1859). One of his biographers calls him "the inspired idiot," although actually he was far from being an idiot. He simply had a poor, slow, plodding mind. This was one of his "givens." But another was his great faith in, and love for, Jesus Christ. As the famous priest of the village of Ars, he was probably the most influential Christian of the nineteenth century in France. He was a confessor and spiritual counselor whose fund of wisdom in dealing with the soul seemed inexhaustible. If he had been more clever by nature, could he have grown into this wisdom? It seems most unlikely. Here is a case where a man offered to God, in simple trust, his bad "given" which was his innate stupidity. God converted this stupidity into wisdom; the bad "given" was made part of a good gift.

Almost every person must be conscious of some such "givens" which seem to doom some of his best aspirations to frustration and failure. There often comes a definite crisis of such self-disillusionment late in childhood or early in adulthood; but this discovery itself—that one cannot transcend these handicaps but must live with them forever—need not burst upon the soul all in one "moment of truth." Some of us cannot remember a time when we did not know our bondage to the "givens."

One can whine about his fate. Or he can use his limitations as an excuse for mediocrity or worse in his own living, saying, "If God had intended me to live better He should have given me better equipment." Or one can stolidly endure it. Or one can take the bad "givens" as a sign that God has prepared for the soul that loves Him such good things as pass man's understanding.

The discovery of our own insufficiency is by no means, of course, the discovery of God's sufficiency for us; but it can be such a prebeginning.

CHAPTER IV

Orphanhood

WE HAVE NOTED that there are people who, having learned the unhappy facts about human love—that it is faulty and it must die—resign themselves as best they can to life in a world where love is at best a poor, evanescent flame of futility. They accept as inexorable the lot of orphans in a world which has no heart for orphans. We noted further that those who do not stop at this point of disillusionment may go on to the knowledge and love of God.

Which of these two courses the soul will take is the result of a deep decision which is made in the crisis of orphanhood. This is the crisis of the soul discovering that the human love by which it has hitherto lived is insufficient. The person in the grip of this crisis knows that he was loved into life and sustained in life by the love of others for him.* But he has learned that this love is by no means what he had trusted it to be, either in quality or reliability. And now he must make up his mind about it.

* One may take the cynical view that most babies are accidents even if born within wedlock, rather than the planned-for creatures of a conjugal love which was set upon giving them birth. But in any case the child, once conceived, must be sustained in life by its mother—and this nurture of the life of the beloved is love, as we are using the term.

The question before him is: Did this love which created and has sustained him thus far originate in his parents, or did it come ultimately from a higher source? It was his very life line as a dependent infant. But if it began in, and ended with, his parents, it was a purely biological factor and a temporary necessity of nature, nothing more. When his mother is gone, her love is gone. Or did this love come to him from beyond the natural order, directed and channeled to him by some benevolent supranatural Power or Person?* If so, this Source of the love remains, and must be what It has always been, and evermore shall be. Its very nature is to give love and help to Its human creature who cannot otherwise live.

It may be objected that this spiritual reflection upon the provenance of love which, I say, accompanies this crisis of orphanhood, has in fact no such structure in the mind of the ordinary person. I seem to be making every child a theologian and metaphysician at that unhappy crisis in his life. This objection strikes me as reasonable; in fact, it occurs to me too! But in answer to it two things may be said. First, the human soul does find the sense of aloneness in the world troubling and oppressive; and this sense comes to very many, I would say most, normally sensitive and intelligent adolescents. A kind of morose melancholy is commonly found in the youth of fifteen

* Somehow it seems to me more likely that the soul thinking naturally, unprompted by others, for the first time, about the possible supranatural Source of love and help, would think of It in impersonal terms, as a Force, a Power, an It. The possible personality of the divine Source would be an afterthought. But this purely personal feeling merits no more than this footnote, since it has no direct bearing upon the outcome.

who was formerly an uncommonly jolly child. He can't tell you, or himself, why he feels this way. I suggest that it is at least partly because he has discovered the insufficiency of the love of his parents for him. They may be excellent parents, as human parents go. But he used to be sure that their love was perfect and as immovable as the hills of Zion; he knows better now, and he is troubled. He has entered upon this critical reflection upon the nature and provenance of love—whether he knows it or not. And this is the second thing that needs to be said: that this decisive reflection of the soul, of the essential self, may be largely or entirely subconscious. It is going on so profoundly that the thinker himself is only vaguely aware, or wholly unaware, of it as it proceeds.

The first, and most fundamental and lasting, lesson which the soul learns is that it must be loved if it is to live. This conviction does not diminish simply with the passage of time and the accumulation of experience; if anything, it increases. The child sees this indispensable love as human, most specifically parental. Then, for reasons we have noted, he learns that it is not enough for his needs. At this point, and to fill the void created by this disillusionment, the hunger for God appears. It may not be a conscious hunger, that is, conscious of its object. The God-hunger is unlike all other hungers, such as those for food, sex, companionship, *et al.*, in that it is indefinite where they are definite; characteristically, it does not know what, or whom, it wants, at any rate in its first stage. It is the vague, aimless restlessness and *Weltschmerz* which arises out of the sense of spiritual orphanhood, of being bereft of love.

This seems the right point to bring into consideration a great promise of Jesus, recorded in the fourth Gospel (St. John 14:18). It is astonishing to me that all of the modern, and older, translators of this verse into English fail to give us the very literal translation, because it would be better than any other. Such a translation would run: "I will not leave you orphans; I am coming to you." Jesus is speaking here to this desolate condition of man, in his hunger for a Lover, Helper, and Protector whose love is as tender as a mother's but is also pure, inexhaustible, and immortal. Lacking such love, we are orphans. "I will not leave you orphans," Christ says. "Rather, I come to you." By His coming to us and abiding with us He delivers us from this orphanhood.

Later, we shall take up for serious consideration this claim of Christ to be able to deliver us from the misery and anxiety of orphanhood. Now we shall analyze further and define as clearly as we can the condition itself. And I must in honesty ask aloud, in the presence of my readers: Am I raising a false issue here—or, if not a false issue, at least a peculiarly private one, my own and perhaps that of some others, but not everyman's? I don't know. I hear some other people now and then speak of their sense of aloneness in such a way that I get the impression they are talking about this spiritual orphanhood which results from the soul's disillusionment with human love received, but whether this is the true cause and nature of their malaise I can only speculate. This is all in truth that anyone can do. I believe in my guess, and it has been made before me by much wiser and deeper seers. That man is deeply lonely, and that he is troubled by his sense of isolation and desolation, really needs no more proof than man's usually desperate effort to deny or suppress the fact. This effort we see in his fatuous endeavor—in every age and situation, in Pericles' Athens no less than in Johnson's America—to drown solitude in "togetherness." Only a very lonely creature, who cannot tolerate his loneliness, sings pep songs about how "the more we get together, the happier are we!" All our manifold ways of "getting together" are a whistling in the dark, an attempt to deny, to disguise, to forget the soul's frightened solitude. This truth is fairly obvious to all who are willing to face it; but the cause and nature, hence the cure, of this condition is by no means so obvious. My theory is only one, and certainly not the only one. Even if this theory does not explain the whole truth of the mysterious matter, it may well explain a large part of it, and because I am sure that it does I now proceed with it.

When true to himself and honest with himself, man usually sees that he is not autonomous. He knows that he is created, not self-creating; dependent, not independent; an effect, not a cause; but while seeing this he sees something else: his own personality. Being a person, he feels superior to all *things* as mere things. Therefore he deeply resists any idea that he may be the product or creature of any impersonal forces. One cannot be the child of any *thing*, and he insists that he either is somebody's child or he ought to be. So man has a two-fold sense of *createdness and sonship*. It should not be claimed for this sense that it is knowledge, or the direct and infallible vision and perception of the truth about man. I make no such claim for it. My claim is that this sense is about as universal as any such human "sense" can be, that it is very human, very natural, and an important part of man's spiritual anatomy.

This sense we are thinking about is partly a feeling and partly a desire. It is a feeling of createdness combined with a desire for sonship. And as it grows in a human life, which it does in the normal course of time and events, the soul grows more and more aware of its need for a God who is both Creator and Father—that is, both Source of being and Source of love.

But does the fact that man *feels* created, and *wants* a Father-God, prove anything more than that he has this feeling and this desire? Does it prove that such a God exists? Dr. Freud, in a famous essay, charges that theistic religion is "a universal, obsessional neurosis of mankind."[1] God, he argues, is only the product of man's wishful thinking and fantasy. Freud simply and uncritically assumed that once it can be shown that man *wants* God it should be self-evident to any intelligent man that God exists only in man's hope and desire. Many people of today follow Freud in this assumption. It is bad logic and bad philosophy. It is certainly true that our wanting something to be true does not make it true; but it is at least as true that our wanting it does not make it false. I want to speak to this personally. I don't think that every single one of my desires is meant to be satisfied. I am sure that it is much better for me that they are not. But I am persuaded to the depths of my soul that every one of my major, basic, fundamental desires is meant to be satisfied—that there is in this world a satisfaction provided for them. A desire can be satisfied only if there is an object, both real and available, which can satisfy it. If one of my primal desires must go unsatisfied, I am sure that it is because somehow I am being blocked or cheated, and not because its object does not exist. I believe that here I speak not for myself only but for man as man. He doesn't really expect to get everything he wants, but he thinks he is meant to get what he most deeply wants and needs. The desires for food, drink, sex, beauty, a sense of meaning in life, human companionship, and other such primary desires, plainly point to the actual existence of food, drink, sex, etc. Man lives by this indomitable faith, this innate vital assurance that his primal hopes are not liars.

When we become aware of our hunger for love and help from above, we should accept it in the same way and with the same tolerance that we accept our other desires, such as those we have just mentioned. A man is not ashamed of his desire for food or human companionship. Why should he be ashamed of his desire for love and help from above and beyond himself? If he is, it is because his thinking has been infected by the Nietzschean virus, the doctrine that only slaves and cowards—to whom, since Freud, may be added neurotics—want the Father-God who can love and help them. It is not at all unlikely that you who are reading this have somewhere along the line picked up this bug. If so, ask yourself if you think it is weak, cowardly, or neurotic to want love and help from other human beings. If that is your belief, I don't know what to say to you. But if it is not your belief, if you think that it is quite all right to want love and help from other people, ask yourself why, then, you feel that it is quite all wrong to want love and help from the only Being who, by definition, is really capable of giving you all the help and love you need.

If you think your basic desires, like those for food, family, health, pleasure, and such, are meant to be satisfied, why should you make an exception of your desire for such help and love as only God can give? If somewhere in this world there is food for the hungry man, is it not at least as likely that there is a Father for the orphan? I am not offering this as any kind of proof of the existence of God. I am only appealing to you to deal sensibly and kindly with your sense of orphanhood and your desire for help and love. What are the facts about it? It is your desire, it is what you want, as truly as are those other deeper desires of yours. It expresses a real need. You may be able to get along without beer, a yacht, a harem, or the ability to read; you cannot get along without help and love. Your desire for help and love may point toward its own fulfilment in God, thus serving you as a guide toward truth, life, and infinite satisfaction of all your desires. The thirsty man's desire for water does not deceive him as to what he needs. It fairly screams at him: "water!"—not "poetry!" or "sex!" All your other essential desires prove to be true and faithful guides, if you have the wit and the will to follow them. Why trust the others but not this one?

I hope I have been able to convince you that, at the very least, your desire for help and love and your longing for a Father do not prove you to be a slave, a weakling, a coward, or a neurotic.

CHAPTER V

Sin

THE INFANT HAS NO sense of sin, of moral failure; but he will grow up into it as surely as he will grow up into conscious sexuality, pride, ambition, fear, or any other badge and sign of membership of the human race.

There are some questions about sin which we need not answer, or even face, in our consideration of the dark mystery, but some facts about it must be noted:

The sense of sin is normal in life. I think it necessary to say this in any discussion of the matter today, because so much is said to the general effect that there is something abnormal and unhealthy about the sense of sin. The term "guilt-feeling" is actually applied to a psychic sickness. I am not questioning the propriety of this; if one's guilt-feeling is obsessive it is a sickness. But there is a healthy and sound guilt-feeling one can have; one gets it by being in fact guilty! This guilt-feeling, I am saying, any normal, healthy person has. And he has it because he earns it by being guilty.

The sense of sin is something we grow up into, regardless of whether our elders actively promote the process. This growing away from our original innocence is a part of our growing up.

The sense of sin is healthiest and does the most good

when sin is understood as a "missing the mark"—which is precisely the meaning of the Greek word for sin, hence the word normally used in the New Testament. Our sense of sin can be an unhealthy and harmful thing if we think wrongly about sin—which is a deplorably easy mistake to make. If our thinking about sin leads either to a flippant carelessness about it or to despair, it is bad thinking. But if our sense of sin is a sense of not having measured up to our capabilities, or of having missed the mark or lost our way, it is good for us—or it will be good for us if we heed it and let ourselves be guided by it. The Greek word for sin—*hamartia*, "missing the mark"—was probably drawn from archery. The boy learning to use the bow would shoot at a target, and he would miss the mark. This was his "sin." He made some mistake in his action; he must see his mistake in order to get rid of it. Thus by correcting his "sinning" he became capable at last of hitting the mark.

I must add in all honesty my conviction as a Christian that there's a lot more in sin than just a well-meaning, amateurish "missing the mark." But insofar as sin is a missing the mark, a failure, a falling short, it is something that can be part of the "preparation of the Gospel" in our lives. A healthy sense of sin convinces us that we need loving forgiveness, and loving help. Who but God can give us this, in the measure of our need?

The sense of sin—again, if it is healthy and sound in us—makes us humble, and only the humble soul can receive God's grace and be open and receptive to the overtures of His love. Could we be humble, hence open to God, if we were without sin? I have no doubt that we should be infinitely more so; but in fact none of us is in that happy state. Every one of us is either a humble and contrite sinner or a proud and defiant sinner. Only the humble can receive the healing love of God; and if our sense of sin melts our pride, as it should, it prepares us for the knowledge and love of God by destroying our resistance to Him.

Matthew Arnold had this to say: "Sin is not a monster to be mused on, but an impotence to be got rid of. All thinking about it, beyond what is indispensable for the firm effort to get rid of it, is waste of energy and waste of time." I quote this for the truth there is in it, and not because I think it is the whole truth about sin, for I certainly do not. We do experience sin as "an impotence to be got rid of." Suppose that you detest lying, but you catch yourself lying at almost every opportunity. It is your *impotence* to shake the habit that troubles you most and of which you are most aware. Self-convicted impotence cries out for love and help from Omnipotence, if haply such love and help may be found.

"There is a shame that bringeth sin; and there is a shame which is glory and grace" (Ecclesiasticus 4:21). We cannot be absolutely sure as to what "Jesus, son of Sirach" (2nd cent. B.C.) meant by this arresting dictum, but we know that there is a shame which only confirms the sinner in his sinning by reducing him to self-contempt. To lose all our self-respect is to lose our will and resolution to overcome the sin that has brought shame to us. And there is a shame which is "glory and grace" because it makes a person realize how important he is to the almighty God of the universe. I cannot trace the process by which the soul moves from this "gracious and glorious"

shame to this awareness of being infinitely—and awfully
—precious to God. But implicit in the process seems to be
this line of reasoning: God is tormenting me for my sin
through my conscience, because He cares too much for
me to sit by and watch me destroy myself. Shame is the
beginning of our redemption if we see it, interpret it, and
act upon it as a *gift of God*. A strange "gift" perhaps, this
torment! Yet, rightly understood, it is a call, a summons,
to turn from misery and self-destruction to life—from
what the Prayer Book calls "the death of sin" to "the life
of righteousness." Shame is given to us as, literally, a life-
saver. It helps dispose the soul to a most ardent love of
God whenever it is seen, welcomed, and acted upon as a
loving gift of a God who cannot endure the sight of us
defiling and destroying ourselves as we do when we sin.
Perhaps we should note here in passing that sin is never
either serious or trivial because *we* think it so. Sin is what
it is because God knows it to be so.

If our mind and attitude toward sin is right, we see God
as our accepting Father and our creative, or recreative,
Helper, and so we are drawn more lovingly to Him. To be
sure, God is "of purer eyes than to behold evil" (Habak-
kuk 1:13), so that the godly man must cry, "If thou, Lord,
shouldest mark iniquities, O Lord, who shall stand?"
(Psalm 130:3). But God does more than to mark our
iniquities, and He does not mark them for reprisal. He
marks them, and invites us to mark them with Him, for
treatment and cure: that He and we may go to work together to destroy these works of the Devil. It is partly
through this working partnership of the grace-giving God
with the grace-receiving sinner that the godly man is

given to see, as he never could see otherwise, the sheer adorable beauty of God. This is the meaning of St. Augustine's paradoxical joy in man's original sin, which he calls *O felix culpa!* It is a "happy fault," not in itself, but in its consequences. Because man has sinned, he must be lovingly accepted and forgiven; in being forgiven he is given to see the ineffable glory of God, whose name is love. St. Augustine was by far too sound a theologian, and too wise a man, to suppose for a moment that sin, any sin, can ever be good in itself. But if sin is followed by repentance, and repentance is followed by God's forgiveness, God has used the evil of sin as an instrument of His omnicompetent love and goodness. Whether the soul might arrive at this vision of God's beauty without having to do it by the hard way of sinning and repenting is, for us, an entirely academic question. We know nobody in the flesh who is without sin and who might therefore show us what is possible to a sinless person. Since the question is thus purely academic I feel no obligation to hazard an answer, this not being an academic book.

We come, most of us surely if not all of us, to a crisis in which we see our moral frailty. Perhaps it is better to speak of it as frailty or insufficiency rather than as impotence, since this last term seems to suggest a total lack of "potency." We don't as a rule see ourselves as complete moral bankrupts. After all, a complete moral bankrupt would lack even the decency to see his own bankruptcy, and we aren't quite that badly off. The Calvinist theologians have spoken of total depravity. Most of us do not think that this is our condition. Our real condition, we think, is better described by saying that "the spirit is willing, but the flesh is weak": and in so thinking we are right, I believe. We may call it, then, our weakness, our insufficiency to live up to our own standard for ourselves by the moral sweat of our own brow.

It is easy and cheap to say that every normal person starts with a naturally high opinion of himself. I used to consider this one of the most incontestable of axioms. After a half-century of living with myself and with my fellow men I have come to believe that this "axiom" as it stands is flatly false. It becomes true only if revised to read: "Every person has a naturally high opinion of his ideal self—of the person he wants to be and believes he is meant to be." To say that the ordinary duffer sees himself as a peer of the archangels, or even as being very much better than he actually is, is simply untrue as well as uncharitable. All generalizations about the "ordinary" man and how he "ordinarily" sees himself are dangerous, yet necessary. Let us then make it as personal as we can and think about ourselves. In your reveries do you see yourself as a regal being, in your moral and spiritual character? Then do you turn from that vision of your ideal self to your actual self, and inwardly weep at the contrast? If this is your experience, you may understand that it is the truly normal experience of the person whom God is interiorly preparing and educating for a closer walk with Himself.

We began this chapter on sin by looking at sin as a missing the mark. When the Greeks made this their very word for sin they noted that a person grows in wisdom and strength of character in a way similar to an archer's growth in skill—by noting his mistakes and correcting them as promptly and thoroughly as possible. And they probably noted also that when a boy learning archery has two assets—one, a powerful desire for excellence, and the other a fine teacher—a deep love commonly develops between teacher and pupil, a love born somehow of their joint striving to overcome his "sins" as a neophyte in archery. So, then, *hamartia*, "missing the mark," became the word for sin. Mark now the parallel in the growth and nurture of the soul. We see our ideal selves, we shoot at that mark, and we fail miserably. This is our *hamartia*. Insofar as our sin is our unskillfulness, clumsiness, missing the mark, failing, in our effort to be our ideal selves, it is like the young archer's mistakes: it drives us to our divine Master for help. Our divine Master proves to be the perfect teacher. On the one hand, He will not let us settle for anything less than a perfect performance. This perfectionism is of the essence of good teaching in any teacher, human or divine; but with all His uncompromising demandingness, our divine Teacher is always gentle and patient with us so long as He sees that we are doing our clumsy but earnest best.

Since we are thinking specifically of those experiences in life which can lead us to, and confirm us in, the knowledge and love of God, I feel constrained to repeat a warning voiced earlier. We must see our sin rightly if it is to bring us closer to God and not to alienate us from Him. There are two temptations, always. The one is to presumption, the other to despair. If we yield to the first, we conclude that God doesn't care a damn what we do; if we yield to the second, we conclude that we aren't worth a damn to Him. (I am choosing my words deliberately, and using them reverently.) Both presumption and despair block the soul from loving union with God.

If we see ourselves as clumsy children of God trying to be the persons He wants us to be, but failing and falling and stumbling miserably all over the lot; and if we see God as our unindulgent, uncompromising, unwearying, loving Master who never gives up on us, who is always at hand to help us to overcome every mistake and to outgrow every missing of the mark, we are "treading where the saints have trod" on our way to the conquest, by the power of His grace, of all our faults, and to the perfect knowledge and love of Him.

CHAPTER VI

Fear

ONE OF THE OLDEST of antitheistic slogans is that which explains the origin of the gods ever so simply: Fear creates them. *Timor facit deos.* The tidiness of this theory makes it insidiously attractive—like the Loreley. But the theory comes apart in every which direction as soon as you put it to work on cases. It cannot explain, for example, why fear-ridden man has created so many gods who are themselves more terrible and more to be feared than are those frightening things from which we want the gods to deliver us. If it was fear that drove man to invent such a god as Moloch, it's strange that he should try to get rid of his fears by creating a kind of Ultimate Terror. Man can do some monumentally foolish things, but seldom does he do anything so obviously contrary to his own comfort and obvious best interests.

Yet it is not to be denied that fear plays a profoundly influential role in all religions of salvation. It does not create the gods. Rather, it enhances and intensifies man's sense of need for God. It drives him to God.

And it ought never to be denied by the friends and advocates of theistic religion* that very often, when man

* Some would say that such a phrase as "theistic religion" is really redundant—that if a person is religious he is, of course,

has taken his fears and terrors to God praying to be relieved of them, he has behaved very stupidly and he has not used the mind God gave him. If, let us say, the gentlefolk of a precarious aristocracy fear an uprising of the Helots, it may be that God would love to preserve them from that peril by moving them to do justly and to love mercy. But if their prayer to God says only this—"Dear God, please keep them peacefully in their place!"—it is foolish and it will be fruitless. This may be a rather too obvious example to make my point well; but I often think that God must be both disappointed and appalled by some of our more fearful prayers. In our fear of something we may ask God to preserve or to extricate us without asking Him for any kind of instruction as to what He would have *us* to do to meet the crisis.

Let us shift from the general to the personal and particular mood. We are thinking about *our fears*, not about fear in general. And the first thing we must do is to discriminate between fears which are our friends and fears

---

a theist. This identification of religion with theism has in fact a kind of legal status in this country. In 1890, in the case of *Davis v. Beason*, the United States Supreme Court declared that "the term 'religion' has reference to one's views of his relations to his Creator, and to the obligations they impose of reverence for his being and character, and of obedience to his will." But that was 75 years ago. Today we have among us many who would call themselves "humanists" rather than "theists" in their religion—and would insist that they are every bit as "religious" as are the theists, if not more so! Insofar as they are both religious and humanist, it would seem that they somehow believe in men where the theist believes in God. I use the term "theistic religion" simply to indicate that the kind of religion we are thinking about is God-centered rather than man-centered.

which are our foes. "I will have no man in my boat who is
not afraid of a whale," says Captain Starbuck in Melville's
Moby Dick. The man unafraid of whales will run unnecessary risks on a whaling voyage, thus endangering both
himself and others. Utter fearlessness of whales, snakes,
germs, alcohol, drugs, lies, the acquisitive instinct, false
doctrine, and some other things much too numerous to
mention, is the mark of the fool. Clearly, some of our fears
are gifts of God, whose purpose is to bless and sustain our
lives. A little common sense reflection will reveal to us
which of our fears are in this category of being our
friends.

But there is no sense in pretending that all our fears are
either friendly fears, of the sort we have just noted, or that
they are simply the products of "negative thinking" on our
part. If we are fools, or cowards, for quaking before such
bêtes noires as physical or mental illness, occupational
failure, personal failure, sin, war, loneliness, bereavement,
and death, then fools or cowards we are; but so long as we
acknowledge and confess our fearfulness we are at any
rate not pretenders, as are those who deny their fears.

To grow in wisdom and in factual knowledge is, para-
doxically, to grow in fearfulness, at any rate in fearfulness
of a sort. By virtue of simply learning more and more
about more and more things, we learn more and more
things that are to be feared. The man who knows nothing
actually about the hydrogen bomb may be very much
"braver"—in this case, more ignorantly optimistic—about
our chance of surviving a nuclear war than the nuclear
physicist can be. The latter is afraid because he knows. It
would be easy to illustrate this in a thousand ways. Ten

years ago, not many of us could see much reason for fearing the effect of smoking upon the lungs. We know better today, so we are more afraid.

On looking back over the preceding paragraph I find that the two examples I have given to illustrate how growth in knowledge sometimes means growth in fearfulness have one thing in common: the peril of nuclear war and the peril of lung cancer are both of them open and aboveboard perils. They are perils which by their nature can be effectively faced and disposed of by human intelligence and moral resolution—if we can muster enough of these commodities. The *if* clause here is rather weighty in the balances. But at least it can be said that these two particular evils, nuclear war and lung cancer, are reasonably clear-cut, visible, and diagnosable to us. What of those more "nameless" fears, as we sometimes call them: the fears to which we cannot assign a definite known cause, or which speak to us of evils beyond our, or any mortal's, power to overcome?

Not only does the number of our fears multiply as we grow in knowledge and experience; we grow also in the awareness of our insufficiency to cope with the evils which threaten us. Our fears grow more and more numerous, our self-confidence grows less and less—if it may be said that anything grows down instead of up. Fearfulness becomes a fixed state of mind and condition of the soul; vague and indefinite, but deep, haunting, and troubling. Such is the normal state of man—of the mature, healthy man, we may add, not simply of the neurotic or the misfit. Why are so many books written, and evidently read, on

the subject of overcoming our fears? Our question answers itself.

Now, the godly people we meet in the Bible and the
saints whom we meet throughout the Christian era confess and reveal this fearfulness in themselves quite clearly.
But they confess and reveal something else: that through
firm self-commitment to God, the servant of the Lord receives supernatural courage and strength to see him
through all the worst that man or devil can do to him.
Sings the Psalmist: "The Lord is on my side; I will not
fear: what can man do unto me?" (Psalm 118:6). "Greater
is he that is in you, than he that is in the world," writes St.
John to beleaguered Christians (I John 4:4).

King David is not presented to us in the Bible as some
kind of superman of whom it could be said, as Kipling
says of Gungha Din, that "he didn't seem to know the use
o' fear." There is an instructive passage (I Samuel 30:1-6)
about how the king was once thoroughly frightened and
how he dealt with the fear. After a disastrous military
reverse and massacre, his own people spoke of stoning
him, and this was an ominously strong possibility. Then,
we read, "David encouraged himself in the Lord his God."
We are not told precisely how. But he was much too
shrewdly realistic, and too genuinely godly, to suppose
that he could somehow manipulate God to prevent the
catastrophe. His encouraging himself in the Lord must
have consisted rather of reminding himself of God's promises never to forsake the soul who trusts in Him. Even if
God should allow him to be slain, yet would David trust
in Him. This kind of trust in God's goodness which makes
no demands of God, which does not try to force God's

hand, which simply trusts that God in His loving wisdom will do something better than His servant can dream of, somehow makes a man more than master of his own fears.

I can't always in good conscience speak well of the Calvinistic tradition of Christianity, but I can unreservedly agree with one writer who notes with admiration the powerful confidence in God which is to be found in the Calvinists of the classic type. In the war for the liberation of the Netherlands, after the terrible siege and fall of Haarlem, that doughty Calvinist the Prince of Orange wrote in 1573 to Diedrich Sonoy, lieutenant governor of the province of North Holland:

> You ask if I have entered into a firm treaty with any great king or potentate, to which I answer, that before I ever took up the cause of the oppressed Christians in these provinces, I had entered into a close alliance with the King of kings; and I am firmly convinced that all who put their trust in Him shall be saved by His almighty hand."[1]

The Calvinist Christian has no monopoly of this confidence in God. The reason it is so commonly found in Calvinists is their conviction of the absolute sovereignty of God, and this conviction is one which any believing Christian shares. The sense of God's sovereignty is the sense of His invincible rule, dominion, and control of all things past, present, and to come—in heaven, on earth, and even in hell. *God will have His perfect way with everybody and everything*: this is the meaning of His sovereignty. If we believe this, while believing also in His perfect love, there is born in us that confidence which speaks in St. Paul's words: "Our light affliction, which is but for a moment, worketh for us a far more exceeding and eternal weight of glory; while we look not at the things which are seen, but at the things which are not seen . . ." (II Corinthians 4:17-18).

Our fears speak to us of things that can hurt or destroy us. Our faith in God, if it is Christian faith, does not produce in us any illusion that the things we fear aren't really there, or that they aren't as bad as they seem. For all we can ever tell at a given moment, they may be even worse than they seem; and we know that there are always some things present and at work which we should fear if we could see them, which we cannot. True faith changes none of this.

The people of the Bible and of the Jewish-Christian tradition, whose faith is in the living God, do not look to God to "save" them by removing all, or any, of these ugly and threatening things from their path. They know that He may do so in fact, and they are not reluctant to ask Him to do so—if it be possible, if it be His holy will; but their confidence lies not in any hope or expectation that He will remove their obstacles or enemies. Rather, they encourage themselves in Him as David did, by remembering that after "the flood of mortal ills" has done its worst they will behold the rainbow of His covenant; in the aftermath of the terror they will look back upon the travail of their souls and be satisfied that in all things God was working with them for good.

CHAPTER VII

Grief

"HALF THE INTEREST of my life seems to have gone when I cannot look forward any more to his clear voice of welcome or to the letters which were my greatest happiness. For now there is no one to venerate, no one to work for, or to think about while working. I always knew that I was leaning on these feelings too much, but I could not try to prevent them; and so at last I am left with a loneliness that can never be filled."

These mournful words were written by one man of rare mind and spirit about another—by George Romanes about Charles Darwin, after the latter's death. They express grief unmitigated and unsoothed by any consolations of faith or philosophy. This is pure grief, and we begin our consideration of grief as a factor in the life of the soul by analyzing it.

Grief as a universal human experience is normally, though not always, the consequence of bereavement by death. A parent might grieve when his child goes off to another side of the globe to seek his fortune, with little prospect of ever returning home. In any event, the proximate cause of grief is separation. Grief is the anguish of devastating personal loss, the kind of loss which makes the griever feel painfully crippled or pitiably alone, or both. This is poignantly expressed by Romanes in the passage quoted above.

In one respect, Romanes' grief for Darwin was untypical of grief in general, in that Romanes and Darwin were quite untypical men. They were not only friends, but colleagues and partners in scientific research on a very high intellectual level. They were geniuses; and we who are not geniuses tend to feel that geniuses do nothing and feel nothing after the manner of the rest of us. Even their grieving must be different from ours. This is not entirely false. A man like Romanes knows how immeasurably poorer our whole world must be for the loss of a Darwin. Only the death of a great creative genius seems to entail that loss to the whole world, causing us to cry that there hath passed a glory from the earth—from the whole earth. And sometimes only another genius can properly assess this loss to the world. I think this was true of Darwin at the time of his death, and so I say that we must view Romanes' grief as being, in this one particular, untypical and exceptional, but this is only the exception that proves the rule. What comes through to us so powerfully, clearly, and movingly from Romanes' soul is his sense of a "loneliness that can never be filled" now that Darwin is gone. And this is the universal essence of grief, this personal loneliness enhanced, or embittered, by the sense of the irreplaceability of the beloved.

It is an unusual person who can get through childhood without experiencing grief. A child's grief at the death of a pet is authentic grief. If ever you have tried to comfort the child with the promise of another puppy or kitten, you may have noticed that the comfort may prove strangely ineffective, for he may reply: "There just can't be another Rags!" And so there can't. Grief can never be exorcised or even mildly assuaged by the promise of a replacement of the irreplaceable lost one.

Like any other mortal woe, such as sickness, pain, or poverty, grief has no inevitably strengthening or ennobling effect upon the soul, and this is a reminder which can hardly be repeated too often. Some life philosophies make a golden text of Aeschylus' *pathein mathein*—"to suffer is to learn." Christianity does not. Christians who believe that grief somehow strengthens, purifies, or drives closer to God the person who experiences it are believing this all on their own; it is not *de fide*. Moreover, their belief is, I think, wrong. If the grief-stricken person is strengthened and sanctified, it is by his faith and by God's grace—not by his grief itself. We may put it this way: If a person has no faith whatever in God, no belief in God's goodness and loving purposes at the time he suffers grief, it is a mistake to suppose that his grief will in some strange way create in him a faith which wasn't there before. Why should it? How could it? The truth is rather that if a person has some faith, some knowledge and love of God when grief strikes, the experience will strengthen and deepen his union with God. We can see how this comes about. With his prior trust in God he believes, when the grief is upon him, that the God whose name is love is in full charge of this sorrowful event, because He is God. He may wonder at the time why God permits it; the bereavement or loss may strike him as not only tragic but senseless. If the one who is loved and lost was a promising young man, or a young mother whose children need her, it doesn't make sense. This may well be the initial reaction to grief of the stricken faithful soul. But his question is a question, not a rebellion or a denial or even what would constitute in the diplomatic world "a strong protest." The faithful person raises his question about whether the bereavement "makes sense" precisely because he is faithful, and knows that God has the answer to his question—and that this answer will be good, being God's answer.

Faith is loving receptivity and openness to God. He who has it can listen and hear when God speaks. And God speaks to the grief-afflicted soul His healing and life-giving word, through the listener's faith, love, and knowledge born of previous experience. What the grieving soul needs to receive in its momentary anguish is the assurance of certain truths which it already knows, but of which it tends to lose sight when death or separation strikes. It must learn anew that the beloved was God's child. We so readily say that "our" child or parent or friend was "taken from us" as if he actually were ours, to have and to hold on our terms regardless of God's will for him. The faithful person sees his own grief as at least partly a disclosure of his false possessiveness. We must go on learning and re-learning throughout our mortal life that our loved one is really God's loved one. If we have enough faith to know and to accept this truth, each successive experience of grief will confirm us in this knowledge and will enable us to say as Tennyson said about Arthur Hallam:

> Forgive my grief for one removed,
> Thy creature, whom I found so fair.
> I trust he lives in thee, and there
> I find him worthier to be loved.

It is clear enough from the lengthy protestations of his poem (*In Memoriam A.H.H.*) that Tennyson, the earnest but dubious Christian, had trouble making his own "trust" stick. None the less, he saw the point: If we truly believe that another person is to be loved "in God" rather than as a being who exists simply by himself and for us, we shall then see that our grief is, among other things, a revelation—and a warning—that we have loved somebody too much "in himself" and too little "in God"; too much for our own sake, too little for God's sake. The cruelest pang of grief is the sense of our own personal loss. The only cure for this is a rebirth in our hearts and minds of the simple truth of the matter—that our pain is not only painful but sinful, insofar as it results from our having claimed as our own a person who is only God's.

There is, then, a selfish element in most, possibly all, of our grieving which needs to be repented and forgiven. And the only person who will or can repent it is he who already has some faith, some knowledge and love of God. Grief can be the means by which God draws a soul closer to Himself, if that soul is already disposed toward God. In such a case, after the bitter pain of the grief at its crisis has passed, the soul enters into the unearthly joy of the consolations of God. I have heard more than one faithful Christian say, in the aftermath of a cruel and devastating bereavement: "He seems closer to me now than he ever did when he was still with me in the flesh." There was no "spiritualism" involved; it was simply a divine assurance that when God gathers one of His children to Himself that person is henceforth and forever not only closer to God, but closer to those who remain in the flesh.

Grief reveals, then, to him who has sufficient faith to see it, this two-fold truth: that we do not own the person whose loss we mourn, and that God, who does own him, loves him—and us—infinitely more than we do. God reveals this to each sufferer in protection to the sufferer's ability to receive it. Augustine was a godlier man for the death of his mother because he had a ready faith. It is ever thus with those who truly believe.

The grief of bereavement serves another necessary purpose in preparing the soul for deeper union with God. It keeps us mindful of the shortness and uncertainty of human life. That portion of Psalm 39 which is appointed to be read at the burial of the dead is not, on the face of it, a cheerful or comforting discourse, with such verses as these:

> Behold, thou hast made my days as it were a span long, and mine age is even as nothing in respect of thee; and verily every man living is altogether vanity.
>
> I am a stranger with thee, and a sojourner, as all my fathers were.
>
> O spare me a little, that I may recover my strength, before I go hence, and be no more seen.

Historically and theologically, of course, these verses are pre-Christian, and express a Hebrew belief about life and death which has in it little hope of immortality. Yet they express also something that Christians, like all men, actually experience in bereavement: this chilling reminder of their ephemerality. It may be asked why it is that this sense of our helpless mortality which accompanies grief does not alienate us from God by moving us to reproach Him for having made us such "frail creatures of dust, and feeble as frail." Any simple explanation of so profound a mystery as this must sound at once presumptuous and jejune, and yet it must be attempted. As I ponder how to attempt it here, some words in the Song of Hannah (I Samuel 2:6-11) come to mind:

> The Lord killeth, and maketh alive: he bringeth down to the grave, and bringeth up.
> The Lord maketh poor, and maketh rich: he bringeth low, and lifteth up.
>
> He raiseth up the poor out of the dust, and lifteth up the beggar from the dunghill, to set them among princes, and to make them inherit the throne of glory: for the pillars of the earth are the Lord's, and he hath set the world upon them.

We have here a classic expression of a universal insight —universal, that is, among people who have some knowledge of the living God, the God of Abraham, Isaac and Jacob, of Elkanah and Hannah, of Jesus and Paul, and of all who call upon His name. This insight is to this ultimate truth: that the very God who manifests His love *obviously to man's sight* by raising the poor from the dust and the virtually dead man to vigorous life and health is the same God who, *no less lovingly but with a most un-obvious love,* "kills" and otherwise "brings low" His beloved children. In the midst of his afflictions Job showed this insight, at least for a moment. When his wife suggested that he curse God and die, he answered, "What? Shall we receive good at the hand of God, and shall we not receive evil?" (Job 2:10).

The Christian reader of the last paragraph is by now protesting that, however things may have seemed to such Old Testament, pre-Christian worthies as Hannah and

Job, no Christian should slander God by saying that we receive "evil" as well as "good" at God's hands. I agree. And I think it at least possible that Job or Hannah would agree, if they could sit down with us and analyze these words "good" and "evil" and their immediate and ultimate implications. What true faith must believe about this is that anything God does is good, but we may not see it as good. When we call something evil we mean that we don't like it, it is a hindrance to our happiness and to our welfare so far as we can see.

It is pre-eminently in our grief of bereavement that our faith, such as it is, enables us to see what God would gently and lovingly show us—that we simply do not have the knowledge of good and evil; not ultimately. This knowledge belongs to God alone. What we so readily— and, in terms of our human relativities, so rightly—call "evil" may well be a pure good, or it may at least be the necessary means and instrument of an ultimate good, in whose goodness we ourselves shall one day be full and joyous partakers. To see this, to believe this, one must have some faith. This is granted; but when grief puts our faith to the test and spurs it into action the resulting movement of the soul is toward a clearer knowledge and a deeper love of God.

CHAPTER VIII

Beginnings

WE HAVE BEEN THINKING about those common human experiences which can, and often do, serve to quicken and to deepen in the growing soul a desire for God. Such experiences constitute a kind of individual, psychological Preparation of the Gospel. I have assumed that every reader has shared in some or all of these experiences—the sense of orphanhood, guilt, fear, etc. We could prolong this phase of our discussion by reflecting upon other experiences which tend to have the same effect of driving, or predisposing, the soul toward God. But this book can't be all preparation—not even all Preparation of the Gospel. We remember the bear cub, in the children's parable, who asked his mother how one learns to walk. He was well advised to set his paws on the ground, to quit talking and to start walking. This is good advice not only to bear cubs. So we take a turn at this point, from the prebeginnings to the beginnings of the active life of realized union with God.

*   *   *

This union with God, into which a man can enter at any moment and to which we are called, is a union of mutual love and knowledge between God and His child. Let's try at this point to be very clear about what is involved here, and what is not. A personal union between any two persons is not a merger. In holy matrimony, we say, two persons are made "one flesh." This term is a mystical one, not mathematical. John and Mary, made sacramentally and mystically "one flesh," remain the two persons, John and Mary; they are not made a single person John-Mary.

Likewise, union between God and His human child is not merger. When you enter this union you do not cease to be your individual self. On the contrary, you may confidently look forward to being changed from your present imperfect self into your true, best, and full self, in God's good time and way.

This fact of the nature of personal union is a blessing, or God would not provide it. But there must come moments along the way, in the course of the realization and working out of the union, when the human partner is bound to regret it. Here again the analogy of marriage is helpful. The old adage about how the course of true love never runs smoothly is true, and its truth obtains between God and His child no less then between man and wife. God wants something to be done in one way, and I, His human child and junior partner, want it another way. How much easier, less tense and trying, the divine-human union would be if it were merger, not union; if in it man would be simply absorbed by God—or God by man! Then there would be no clash of wills, since there would be only one will.

It is necessary, I think, that this fact about the union be squarely faced and knowingly accepted from the beginning, to prevent disappointment or possible bitter disillusionment later on. It is good when a person weary of conflicts with other people who have minds and wills of their own turns to God for "peace," or for whatever he feels most need of when he turns. But if he is seeking a friend and companion who will never talk back to him he had better not look for such an accommodating friend in God.

There is a kind of religion which has been very popular in America for years, and continues to be, which may be called "peace of mind" religion. I will mention no names of the priests and prophets of this religion and I have no desire to speak of it unkindly. Those of us who are disturbed, as I confess I am, by the popularity of this cult should try to understand it. Clearly, very many of us want, and are hungrily looking for, "peace of mind"; if it were not so, the temples of this cult would be empty. What is it, then, that we want, when we say that we want God to give us "peace of mind"? As I cast about for an answer, I recall a friend and former parishioner who came to church some years ago on the first Sunday after Trinity. The Holy Gospel for that Sunday is our Lord's parable of the rich man who went to hell and the poor man who went to heaven (St. Luke 16:19-31). I preached on this passage, my sermon being essentially an exposition of the story itself. My friend was profoundly troubled after the service. He did not accuse me of saying anything in the sermon that was not implicit in Christ's story, but it wasn't the kind of thing he came to church for, he said. I asked what he did come to church for, and he answered instantly: "For peace of mind. We live in a world of troubles. When I worship God I want to get away from it all." Isn't this in fact what we have in mind when we think of "peace of mind" for ourselves—"getting away from it all"? And, along with this, entering some kind of blissful nirvana, here and now, in which no other will gets in the way of our own will; this, for me at least, would be "peace of mind."

I am saying that people quite understandably want this, and since you and I are people we might as well say straight out that we want it. Moreover, our desire for it may turn us toward God, and if it does He will graciously receive us, no matter what our motive or "angle" in turning to Him may be. But we must understand that whereas God offers us *peace*, He does not promise us "peace of mind" as we have defined it. The peace He gives may be an infinitely more blissful peace than any "peace of mind" could possibly be, but it is different, and we should mark well the difference to prevent any disappointment later on.

The peace of God is not so much a state of mind as it is a total condition of being. It is the state of being at one with God in what we will and strive for, even when this goes against the grain of our self-interest—as it often does. A man in a torment of desire for alcohol, but abstaining because he is an alcoholic and knows that God wants him to abstain, will have the peace of God in the midst of his thirst. It will not be "peace of mind" such as might come from being able to forget that there is such a thing as bottled happiness. The peace of God is not the banishment of all torment of desire and privation. It does, however, have an indescribable, supernatural tonic effect upon the fighting and struggling soul.

Thomas Carlyle spent ten years of constant labor upon

his book on the French Revolution. When the manuscript was completed he gave it to his friend John Stuart Mill for a critical reading. One of the maids of the Mill household thought that the precious manuscript was only scrap paper, and used it to start a fire on the hearth. It was a terrible moment for Mill when he had to tell Carlyle what had happened to the fruits of his ten years' labor. Carlyle turned pale and said nothing. That night he described in his diary the inner side of this desolating experience in these words: "It was as if my Invisible Schoolmaster had torn up my copybook when I showed it to Him and said, 'No, boy, thou must write it better!' " I recall this episode as an authentic example of the peace of God. Carlyle had it—one might better say, it had him—in that bleak moment. He felt the stern, demanding love of the "Invisible Schoolmaster" telling him through his misfortune that he was to write it again, and to write it better. This he proceeded to do.

But what, we may well ask, was the benefit, the advantage, to Carlyle, in having the peace of God in this crisis? After all, it didn't restore the lost treasure to him. It didn't deliver him from the cruel necessity of doing the job all over again. For all we know, it didn't even enable him to sleep better that night. The peace of God provided none of these blessings. Then what good came of it at last? I would answer, two things: a better book and a better man. A better book, I guess; I must guess here, not having read the ill-fated first version. But my guess is based on some experience and observation. A book is usually the better for having been completely rewritten. And a better man, certainly. Through this experience Carlyle grew into a deeper awareness of the truth about him and about every man: that he cannot control fate or master destiny or even determine events. Only God can do that. But if a man will humbly, faithfully, lovingly, give himself over to the divine Master and Ruler to be a willing servant of the Master's purposes he will be given that peace which, as Matthew Arnold describes it, "man did not make, and cannot mar."

How, then, shall we describe the peace of God? It is a condition of being which results from our acceptance of God's will as our own in such a way that we subject our whole life and striving to the service of His will. This is the human precondition of the peace of God. It comes from God as a gift; and it comes, and is experienced, not as a delicate feeling of pleasant quietude within ourselves but as a power from on high. Here I would quote some telling words of the Swedish bishop and theologian Dr. Anders Nygren:

> We like to imagine that peace is a delicate thing, which we must lock up within ourselves, and protect, and hide in the depths of our hearts, so that it may not be lost or be evaporated. But in the Scriptures peace is spoken of in an utterly different way. There it is said that God's peace is a mighty power, which of itself can keep our hearts and our thoughts. God's peace is a mighty fortress, in which we are well defended and safe against all hostile powers of destruction. It is not we who are to protect peace, but rather it is peace which is to protect us."[1]

The Christian may, and I think must, think of the peace which God gives him as being in two stages. While still in the flesh the Christian is *in via*—on the way. His hope is that he will be at the last *in patria*—in his heavenly fatherland. There will be a peace divinely appropriate to life *in patria*. But he needs another kind of peace while *in via*, a peace which, as Nygren says, is like a mighty power which can preserve and keep him from destruction. What Thomas Carlyle needed most in his hour of desolation was courage to carry on, to start all over again; and along with this some assurance from God that some ultimate good could be brought out of his calamity. This assurance came to him as "No, boy, thou must write it better!" So, God's peace came to Carlyle as renewal of courage and of fighting spirit, as reminder that he was man and not God, as realization that God wanted him to write it better, and as assurance that God was with him in fatherly love and care and would give him a happy issue out of this affliction.

To all of us who are *in via*, the peace of God, when it is given, must come in some such form and way—in order to keep us walking in the way without fainting and failing.

CHAPTER IX

Christic

CHRIST IS NOT a past fact or event. In the minds and lives of His followers He lives, not as a memory but as a Presence, as a living Companion, Helper, and Friend. A biographer of Francis of Assisi writes: "Francis lived with Jesus as though they were contemporaries; as though he were one of his followers. He was always near him."[1] This is misleading. Why the "as though"? Francis, or any other complete Christian, would say, "But we *are* contemporaries. I am one of His followers. I live in Him, and He in me."

To anybody who looks at Him seriously, Jesus is either a Presence or a problem, though He can be both. He is a problem because He can't be accounted for as can any other man. Nothing is more hopelessly irrational than a completely rationalized account of Jesus. H. G. Wells said that He is beyond our small hearts. He is also beyond our little minds. We feel that if we knew all the facts about any other man, say, Alexander or Leonardo or Gandhi, we could explain him. We have no such feeling of rational explicability about Jesus. He is a fact, but a fact beyond our analysis; He can be neither explained nor explained away. The total fact of Jesus is total mystery.

The impact of Jesus upon us is different from that of any other man. This is not to say that He makes the same impact upon all. Not all are attracted to Him; some are repelled. Not all find Him credible; from the beginning to the present some have rejected Him as a deluded megalomaniac. But, whatever our reaction, He does not affect us as does any other man. Above all, He does not come to us as a fellow seeker, a fellow striver, hungering for help and love from beyond and above Himself; He comes to us as one who is Himself from above and beyond. His ineffable divine majesty: this is one side of the truth about Him. But the other side of the truth is that to receive Him is to receive the love of God; to know and to love Him is to know and to love God.

This way of putting it makes it sound so simple that "any child can do it," and perhaps any child can. But for almost any adult this coming to, or receiving, Christ is simple in principle but most difficult in practice. In Russian literature, the peasant of Holy Russia is commonly presented as an astonishing exception to this rule, and he may well have been. If he could read the Gospels, or even if he could not, he was somehow able to enter immediate living contact with the living Christ. Authors like Tolstoy and Dostoyevsky did not invent this Christ-filled peasant as a fiction; they knew him in life. Evidently he had a unique capacity for thinking and seeing with his heart. Our lack of this faculty, or poverty in it, makes our coming to Christ more difficult. Several things explain this. The peasant's religion was all that he had. It is not so with us who are "rich in things and poor in soul." He was uneducated where we are miseducated: our trained approach to anything is merely mental. (This is not to say that we think well, but only to say that we can think in only one dimension.) So, miseducated as we are, we approach Jesus as a possible answer to our questions rather than as a possible lover, helper, and healer of our lives. Vital contact with Him on this purely rational basis is as impossible as would be an understanding of a sonnet of Keats by chemical analysis. I am not saying, of course, that the literate man with a trained intelligence cannot hope to enter saving communion with Christ; I am saying that we cannot see and know Christ except with our hearts. And what I mean by this heart-knowledge will become clear, I hope, as we go along.

We approach and meet Christ in the heart-dimension. He invites us to bring our *hungers* to Him, all of which together make up our hunger for help and love from beyond and above ourselves. The ability to do this is in all of us, but we may have to shake off our false sophistication before we can act upon it.

In the New Testament we may read two passages in which the wrong and the right approaches to Christ are luminously set before us. The first is to be found in St. John 3:1-12. Nicodemus seems strangely modern in his approach. He comes to Jesus seeking answers to questions rather than satisfactions of hungers; and he goes away empty. Undoubtedly he has the hungers for help and love, since he is a man; but he assumes that spiritual hungers are intellectual problems, so he asks for "the answers" rather than for food and drink. His is the wrong way. With Zacchaeus (St. Luke 19:1-10) it is different. This man, who despises himself and is despised by others, hungers to be accepted as a man and a child of God. He looks to Jesus for this acceptance and he gets it. Zacchaeus is probably a sharper, cleverer man than Nicodemus, who is merely an intellectual; but it is not his cleverness which makes it possible for Christ to say "Today salvation has come to this house." It is his hunger, his longing to be accepted as "a son of Abraham" (which is the Jewish way of saying "a child of God"); his hunger for help and love; his instinct to suck—come of age.

Such is the way to the knowledge and love of God through Jesus Christ.

But is it possible today? Zacchaeus could come to Jesus in the flesh. It would seem that we, living nineteen centuries later, can come only to the image or memory of Jesus. So it must be—*if* Christ is only a figure and creature of history. Our heads, thinking independently of our hearts, tell us that this is the case. Our hearts speak otherwise.

Perhaps the most pregnant word spoken about Jesus in the past hundred years is this conclusion of Albert Schweitzer's *The Quest of the Historical Jesus:*

> He comes to us as One unknown, without a name, as of old, by the lake-side, he came to those men who knew him not. He speaks to us the same word: "Follow thou me!" and sets us to the tasks which he has to fulfil for our time. He commands. And to those who obey him, whether they be wise or simple, he will reveal himself in the toils, the conflicts, the sufferings which they shall pass through in this fellowship, and, as an ineffable mystery, they shall learn in their own experience who he is.[2]

When Schweitzer wrote this, as a very young man, he had studied the Gospels exhaustively with his splendid intellect, and all that he could say about Jesus as the result of this research was that "He comes to us as One unknown, without a name"; that is, as a person rationally incomprehensible to us. Why then did he not reject Christianity? Because he knew that there remained open to him another approach to Jesus, and this way he took by acting upon Christ's command "Follow thou me!" and setting himself to the task which he believed Christ willed for him, that of a medical missionary. His mind told him that Christ is a riddle wrapped in an enigma. His heart told him that Christ lives, and can be seen, known, and touched "in the toils, the conflicts, and the sufferings" of loving obedience and discipleship. The supreme significance of Schweitzer lies not in his radical eschatological theories about the person of Christ, but in his rediscovery of the secret of the saints: the secret of how the living Christ can be known, and lived with, today.

"He comes to us . . ." says Dr. Schweitzer. This is a mysterious and haunting fact. Nobody feels that Epictetus or Ikhnaton or the Buddha comes to us; but Christ does. Young Schweitzer felt this, and built his life upon it. We, too, will feel and know Christ's mysterious coming, if instead of reaching toward Him or trying to find Him we simply welcome Him. If we hunger for help and love, we are ready for the coming of Christ; and if from the depth of our being we cry "Come, Lord Jesus!" we are given to know that He is already with us and already helping us.

Our right response to Him is simple, direct prayer—the cry for help and love. Christ answers our cry by saying to us from within our souls: "I am here. You are not deceived. Put your hand in mine, and we will walk together."

The term "Real Presence" is usually associated with the sacramental Presence of Christ in the Eucharist. But it is a terribly harmful theological mistake to try to limit Christ's living Presence upon earth to the altars of His Church or even to the Church as a whole, as His Body. He is present everywhere, and He is redemptively present to any soul who cries "Lord, help me!" All our thinking about His Real Presence should begin at this point of our personal meeting with Him in our crisis of hunger for help and love. (Mark well that I do not say our thinking about His Real Presence should *end* at this point.)

Because what I have been saying about the nature of our meeting with Christ will strike some readers as sheer anarchical individualism and subjectivism, I want now to make clearer just what I am saying, and not saying. I haven't even mentioned the Church in all this. I will now. The Church is none other than Christ's own Body, and He comes to all of us through this Body. The holy Scriptures are themselves "the Church," so nobody meets Christ in the Bible apart from the Church. No man can claim to be one of Christ's faithful if he willfully remains outside the Church. Is this plain enough? What I have been saying is that our personal meeting with Christ in the heart-dimension, in our hunger for help and love, is itself a strictly personal matter, not ecclesiastical or formally sacramental. One of the first lessons Christ teaches His disciple is that he belongs to a family, a household of faith, and that he must take his place with his brothers and sisters. There is, there can be, no Churchless Christianity. But to say that no man can meet Christ except *in* the Church is to deny the Gospel's claim that Christ is the true light who enlightens *every* man (St. John 1:9). The Presence of Christ upon earth is more catholic even than His catholic Church.

One of the great theologians of the Eucharist, Durandus of Troarn in the eleventh century, said of Christ's Real Presence: *Motum sentimus, modum nescimus, praesentiam credimus*—"We feel His activity, we don't know the how of it, but we believe He is with us." This can be said not only of the Christ of the Eucharist, but of the Christ who knocks at the door of every heart wherein dwells an emptiness which hungers for fullness.

CHAPTER X

The Common Salvation

In the New Testament Epistle of Jude is found the phrase "the common salvation." This is Jude's description of Christianity. He means that there is no such thing as a private salvation; and all the New Testament writers agree with him. Each in his own way makes the same point, that to be in Christ is to belong to a family and to share with the other members "the common salvation." Christians of our day are rediscovering the Church. It seems strange that the Church should have to be *redis-covered*, but it is so. Among large segments of Christendom there has been, and continues to be, a feeling that the salvation of a soul is a purely private transaction between God and that soul. We are hardly shocked when we hear somebody say, "My religion is my own affair— strictly a matter between myself and my God!" We can only hope that a day is coming, and soon, when such a statement will be a shocker again.

Our salvation by Christ, by which we mean our receiving from Him that knowledge and love of God which is our eternal life, is a most profoundly *personal* matter, but it is not *private*, and this distinction is of the utmost importance. As soon as we respond lovingly to the love of God in Christ, He instantly makes us aware of our brothers and sisters in Him who share the common salvation. If we lack this awareness of them, our response to Christ has not been one of love. Can we love Him, while despising or ignoring those others for whom He died? "Christians" who reject the Church don't do so really because they can't stand the hypocrites in the Church and they find it easier to worship God amidst His woods and templed hills. They do so, I'm afraid, because each one of them wants to be the only child in the Father's house. Now, in this they are no worse than the faithful churchgoers. Every last one of us wants to be God's only child; that is what ails us. But the Christian who insists upon being a Churchman is, at any rate, trying to do something about his ailment. To reject the Church is to reject one's brethren and fellow sinners in Christ.

The gentle St. John of the Epistles says bluntly: "If a man say, I love God, and hateth his brother, he is a liar: for he that loveth not his brother whom he hath seen, how can he love God whom he hath not seen?" (I John 4:20). Of course, this way of putting it raises a question. May not the fact that we *have* seen our brother, and we know him only too well, make it harder for us to love him? It is easier to love the Chinese coolie whom we have not seen than to love our nasty neighbor who poisoned our dog. St. John would concede this point, I am sure. But I think he would support me in saying that one of the most essential truths of the Christian life is this: that we grow in love only as we strive with all our hearts to love the not-easily-lovable. God gives us brethren in the Church who are indeed made to order for this arduous exercise. This is His doing. He gives us these hard-to-love brethren and commands us to love them. This is part of the treatment. The bores, scoundrels, and hypocrites in the Church are as necessary to our salvation as are Baptism and the Lord's Supper. We may protest that all we want is the knowledge and love of God. He answers that we cannot have this except on His terms; and one of His terms is this requirement that we try to love, learn to love, these hard-to-love brethren.

Because our subject is the knowledge and love of God, a full exploration of the nature of the Church as such is not in order. Yet we must be sure that we are thinking about the same thing. In the Episcopal Book of Common Prayer the Church is defined as "the Body of which Jesus Christ is the Head, and all baptized people are the members" (Second Office of Instruction, p. 290). I venture that ninety-five percent of all Christians would accept this, and this is what we mean when we speak of the Church in this discussion. The important truth for our purpose is the unity of each member with Christ the Head—and so with all the other members. The common salvation consists of sharing the common divine life which flows through the body from the Head. Ours is a shared salvation. We are given the knowledge and love of God, we are saved, as we lovingly and *givingly* participate in this sharing of the love of God in Christ.

It is clear to almost all who think deeply about man that he is a social animal, hence there can be no completeness for him in solitude. The Church is necessary to our salvation, to our completeness in the knowledge and love of God, because of this nature which God has given us. As we have noted, part of our "treatment" is this exercise in loving our unlovable brethren. God says to us in effect: "If you would love me, you must love them." So the Church is, among other things, a gymnasium in which we develop the sinews of the soul by loving the unlovable. But it is not only, or primarily, this. The Church is the home of the Holy Spirit upon earth, and in the Church are to be found the *means of grace*. This is not to say that the grace of God operates only in the Church, or that there are no means of grace outside the Church. It is to say that God provides certain special means and devices for our growth in the knowledge and love of Himself, and He has committed these to His Church.

When Churchmen speak of the means of grace they usually mean in particular the Sacraments, which are indeed means by which God gives to hungry souls the manna of His love. But the Sacraments are not the only means of grace in the Church. We have already spoken of that paradoxical but very real one, the task of learning to love the unlovable in Christ. Then there is worship apart from the Sacraments. There is the Bible, which is not the world's book but the Church's. There is the fellowship of kindred minds as well as of unkindred minds. There is the Church's service of the needy world. All of these means of grace (which are opportunities for growth) vary in excellence from church to church; but however imperfect they may be, any soul can profit from them as he finds them in the nearest church, unless he is too proud to accept them. When we enter the Church in the lowliest and meanest little parish, as hungry seekers and willing givers, we shall find what we seek, for God will fill us.

Some of us are natural Churchmen, with a strong taste for the Church; but many others who have a real taste for God have a real distaste for the Church. Earlier I spoke quite harshly about those who reject the Church out of spiritual snobbery and egotism. Let that stand. But there are others whose motives are better. Among these are people who know enough history to know that the Church as a historical institution has something of a "past," to use the classic euphemism. In countless times and ways Christ's church has seemed to betray its Master and to put Him to an open shame by the sins of its leaders and its people. But they who appeal to history must appeal to the whole of history. Let them ponder the bright mystery of holiness in the Church's saints, and let them note that outside the Church there have been no saints. Having just written the last sentence I can feel the indignation crackling in some readers. How dare I make the assertion that outside the Church there are no saints? Well, I know of none. A saint is a Christian whom grace has raised to such a height and stature in the Christ-life, in the knowledge and love of God, that we other Christians *in via* see him as towering above us in the supernatural virtues of faith, hope, and charity. A saint is not simply an eminently good person. Rather he is a very advanced, proficient Christian. I find no such saints outside the Church. And since the Church's primary business in the world is to take ordinary and sub-ordinary folk and to make saints of them, it may justly be said that the Church's record on this score is not bad; it is very impressive.

Others are troubled not so much by the Church's historic scandals as by its present stodginess and dullness. They think that the knowledge, love, worship, and service of God must be always exciting and thrilling. They do not always find the Church so. Hence they feel let down by the cheap art, the drab-brown architecture, the pedestrian preaching, the syrupy music, the bourgeois membership. And they are right. There is no excuse for mediocrity in the Church, and it is sinful to try to make a virtue of it. People instinctively look for the best in brains, art, music, and spirituality when they enter the Church, and they are entitled to find it there. If they do not, it is the fault and sin of those who humanly are the Church. None the less, it must be said that he who wants communion and fellowship with God outside the Church is seeking salvation on his terms rather than God's. God calls no man to become a mossbacked, hidebound ecclesiastic. He calls every man to take his place in the family life of those who are His family.

Another difficulty which trips up many is their intellectual difficulty with some Church doctrines and practices. A person is not an intellectual snob because he has a mind and wants to use it honestly. Of course, not all Christian bodies known as churches teach and do the same things. But whatever the so-called church, be it Anglican, Roman Catholic, Baptist, or whatever, it will present some intellectual difficulty or another. It should be said without any equivocation or apology that the truths of the great Christian dogmas must ultimately be apprehended not by the head but by the heart. Too many Christian theologians have done their best to hide this truth, as if they were ashamed of it. They have tried to create "systems" which would be intellectually irresistible. They have tried to persuade the seeker that he is a fool if he does not accept the "system." This has put much of Christian theology in the category of philosophy, where it does not belong.

Man lernt nichts kennen als was man liebt, says Goethe: a man understands nothing unless he loves it. Apply this to the Christian dogma which gives the most intellectual offense, the dogma of the Holy Trinity. This dogma is preposterous to the mind which sees it only as a propositional description of Godhead. But the trinitarian faith, that God is one God in three Persons, has come out of, and is sustained by, Christian love for God and experience with God. Knowing that the Father's love creates us, the Son's love redeems us, the Holy Spirit's love strengthens and sanctifies us, we lovingly respond—by adoring the triune Love. *Our doctrine of the Holy Trinity is, purely and literally, an afterthought.* First, we see and experience the triune Love; then, and only then, we think about it and formulate our doctrine.

But why, then, think about it at all, before or after? Because God has so made us that we will think most about what we love most. The love of God is the ground, the source and origin, of all the Christian dogmas; and the God-seeker may be sure that if he will approach the Church's mysteries using love, rather than logic, as the key, the door of undertanding will be open to him. To him this can be said with sure confidence: the Lord of the Church who bids you take your place in His family does not command you to understand all mysteries and all knowledge. As I have loved you, He says, even so ought you to love one another (St. John 13:34). If we enter His Church in humble, hungry, loving response to His invitation, we shall see light at once, and as we continue in this holy fellowship the light will grow.

CHAPTER XI

Grace and Growth

IT IS BY GOD'S GRACE that we grow into, and grow in, the knowledge and love of God. But what is God's grace; how do we get it, and how does it work?

Here is a simple but, for our purpose, adequate definition: *God's grace is His love for us, in healing and life-giving action.*

We get grace simply by receiving it from God. We cannot buy it, we cannot earn it. This greatest of all gifts comes to us with no price tag on it, and because we find this so hard to believe we are prone to miss it altogether. But this is the whole truth of the matter: If we want God's help, His grace, we can get all that we need simply for the asking. Grace is free; absolutely, unconditionally free. But perhaps "unconditionally" is not exactly the right word. St. John Chrysostom reminds us that "grace does not come to men at random, but only to those who want and strive for it." Oscar Wilde, repenting in prison, was led to think deeply about grace, and testified: "He who is in a state of rebellion cannot receive grace, to use the phrase of which the Church is so fond—so rightly fond, I dare say—for in life as in art the mood of rebellion closes up the channels of the soul, and shuts out the airs of heaven."[1] This rebellion of the soul is not necessarily conscious rebellion; it can be a subconscious resistance to change and growth in ourselves. Somebody once wrote some "nonsense" verse which is anything but nonsense, about a caterpillar that did not want to become a butterfly.

> "I do not want to fly," said he,
>   "I only want to squirm!"
> And he drooped his wings dejectedly,
>   But still his voice was firm:
> "I do not want to be a fly!
>   I want to be a worm."

The caterpillar rejecting his destiny represents the soul in rebellion against God. The prospect of growth by grace frightens us. Yet God commands us to come up higher. Before further exploring the workings of grace we must get it clear that there is that in all of us which resists grace even while we hunger for it, a fear of change and growth in our own being. The work of grace is not to change our circumstances for the better, which is what we normally want and ask of God, but to change *us*. My prayer for a hundred thousand dollars is one thing, and I can offer it with ease. My prayer for the grace to become a man who could use this money purely to the glory of God is another prayer entirely, and one which I should find much harder to offer with my whole heart.

We get grace, then, by wanting it, asking for it, and using it.

How does grace work in us? First of all, mysteriously. Warden Lawes of Sing Sing used to tell about one inmate who was serving a life term for first-degree murder. Sing Sing was a barren place at the time of this man's arrival.

After he had been there for a while he asked permission to take on the job of planting trees, hedges, and flowers. This granted, he proceeded to beautify the prison landscape. He was doing more than indulging a taste for horticulture; he was responding to grace. As he transformed the appearance of Sing Sing he was transformed in his own being. The mysteriousness of it lies in several facts. First, that a man capable of his crime should have in himself the longing and the capacity for such change in his being. Secondly, that God should be able to work such a change in such a man under such circumstances. Thirdly, that God should be able to use this man's work as a means of grace to other prisoners, as He undoubtedly did, and continues to do. Mystery and might: these are the two major qualities of God's grace at work.

Grace is mysterious and unpredictable, yet there are some definite channels through which it is given to us. Christians who believe that the Sacraments are divinely appointed means of grace know that they receive God's help through the Sacraments. When Luther was in one of his frequent moods of despondency he would write on his slate "I have been baptized." This was often enough to set him on his feet again. By God's grace he had been adopted as God's child in Holy Baptism, and he needed only to remind himself of this to experience the grace of divine adoption surging up in him and giving strength to his week knees.

An eminent psychologist who was deeply sceptical about religious faith once wandered into a church and sat down to meditate in the stillness. Suddenly a young woman, still a girl, entered the church, and he could see that she was in some dire anguish. She knelt for a while in prayer, then entered the confessional. He was there when she came out, and it was hard for him to believe that she was the same person. Gone was all the torment; she was composed, serene, and at peace. This Sacrament of Absolution can be abused in practice, but she knew how to use it: that is, to receive God's grace through it. Here is a *definite* channel of grace, to which the penitent can go knowing in advance that the promised grace is there waiting for him.

Those who find food for their pilgrimage in the Holy Communion know that God keeps them alive and growing by this means of grace. There are differing doctrines as to how Christ gives Himself to His faithful at the altar, but no one can receive this Sacrament in faith and love without receiving grace to grow in the likeness of Christ. No channel of grace is more definite, more certain and unfailing, than this.

But is it not true that people can receive all the Sacraments without being helped? Indeed so. There is supernatural grace in the Sacraments, but no magic. Their *validity* rests upon the faithful promises of God, but their *efficacy* depends upon our disposition in receiving them, and our disposition must be that of hungering love. The Church's teachers too commonly neglect this one most needful thing as they teach us about the right disposition for receiving the Sacraments. They stress the necessity of faith. I will not say that they overstress this, but rather that they understress something more essential even than faith: hungering love, the longing to be more like Christ and less like ourselves. True love for Christ is longing to be like Him. What can it profit us to have unquestioning faith in the grace of the Sacraments if we are not determined to use that grace for the end for which it is given: growth in Christlikeness?

Our disposition, as we receive the Sacraments or any other means of grace, should be that of hungering love for Christ: a love which longs to be with Him and to be like Him. *This is the only Christian disposition there is.* Any other dispositions we may have in our approach to God are either non-Christian, sub-Christian, or anti-Christian.

This calls for thorough and candid consideration.

All our praying, all our desiring even, is for one or the other of two things outside ourselves, or a change in things inside ourselves. If, for example, we pray for the peace and prosperity of our country, it is for something outside ourselves. I hasten to say that this does not make it wrong or unworthy praying. Our Lord bids us bring to God all our desires, and it is surely right to desire peace and prosperity. Such a prayer is for God's providence. But if, for another example, you are troubled by your bondage to the sin of malice, and you long for a Christlike charity, and you pray for deliverance from that sin and the gift of that virtue, your prayer is for a change in yourself. It is a prayer for God's grace. So we have these two kinds of praying: for God's providence, and for God's grace.

By teaching us to pray for our daily bread, our Lord gives His divine sanction and approval to praying for God's providence. But do not the heathen pray likewise? And let us understand one thing clearly: God could answer all our prayers for His providence exactly as we want them answered, for fifty years, without our growing an inch in the knowledge and love of Him.

There is a strangely provocative text in Psalm 106. The Psalmist is recalling the Israelites in their wilderness wanderings, how they prayed for God's providence and got it. "He gave them their request; but sent leanness into their soul." They wanted food, drink, shelter, protection, victory in battle; God gave them all these, but this did not make them better people, with more knowledge and love of God. They had prayed for providence only, not for grace.

It all comes to this: that we get what we want, what we most deeply and consistently want. This is because God will give us what we want. If we want only the gifts of His providence, these, and only these, we shall have. If with all our heart we want that knowledge and love of Him which is eternal life, this we shall have. Here we should state an equation which is a key affirmation of this book. *The knowledge and love of God, and Christ-likeness, are one and the same thing.* "And this is life eternal, that they might know thee the only true God, and Jesus Christ, whom thou has sent" (St. John 17:3).

In the Gospel and the Epistles which bear the name of John we find a unique understanding of what it means to *know* God. St. John would support me in saying that every Christlike act you perform increases in you that eternal life which is loving union with God. We can make it specific. Suppose that a former friend of yours has done you a great wrong, and some adversity has put him entirely at your mercy. You owe him nothing; you have the old score to settle with him, and one way to do this would be to leave him to the wolves. But you are trying to be a Christian, and you pray for the grace to be a Christian in this crisis. On the morning of the day of decision you are not at all sure that you are up to it, so you go to Holy Communion with a special intention for God's guidance and grace. This is given to you, and you rise to the occasion. Certainly this is not an achievement of heroic sanctity, but you will have grown in the knowledge and love of God and in the eternal life. You will not know more *about* God than you did before, you will know more *of* Him. Since God is love, it may even be said that you have participated in Him.

The pagan Plotinus came close to Johannine Christianity in his concept of knowing God, when he taught that "it is to the gods, not to good men, that our likeness must look; to model ourselves upon good men is to produce an image of an image; we have to fix our gaze above the image and attain likeness to the Supreme Exemplar." The Christian has one immense advantage, in that for him the "Supreme Exemplar" has come down to earth as a man of our flesh in such a way that "our likeness" can look to Him. This is why Luther the Christian can say so much more simply than Plotinus: "Love is an image of God, and not a lifeless image, but the living essence of the divine nature which beams full of all goodness."

When we think of St. Paul's teaching about the knowledge and love of God, the 13th chapter of First Corinthians comes at once to mind. But there is another passage, Romans 5:1-5, in which he is more definite: "Therefore being justified by faith, we have peace with God through our Lord Jesus Christ: by whom also we have access by faith into this grace wherein we stand, and rejoice in hope of the glory of God. And not only so, but we glory in tribulations also; knowing that tribulation worketh patience; and patience, experience; and experience, hope; and hope maketh not ashamed; because the love of God is shed abroad in our hearts by the Holy Ghost which is given unto us." Here is a superb description of the progress of the soul in Christ. St. Paul sees our knowledge and love of God as the cumulative result of our striving to be conformed to Christ in our own being. There are first the tribulations, the hard trials of the Christian who finds that it is simply not in him to be Christlike but who faithfully perseveres in this effort toward the impossible. Out of this travail comes the fighting patience so necessary to the long haul. Then comes the benefit of experience. As this grows, hope grows, and the confident assurance that love's labor is not all for nothing. The end and consummation of it all is our triumphant vision of the love of God which has been our very life all the way through, even though at some moments on our march we saw it only dimly or not at all.

When I spoke a while ago of our loving as a participation in God Himself I came close to the heresy which sees no distinction between the Creator and the creature. Here I return to St. John for authority and support: "No man hath seen God at any time. If we love one another, God dwelleth in us, and his love is perfected in us" (I John 4:12). St. John is not confounding the Creator with the creature. "No man hath seen God at any time." God is the Wholly Other, "dwelling in the light which no man can approach unto; whom no man hath seen, or can see" (I

Timothy 6:16). But if this infinite transcendence of God were the only truth about Him and ourselves, no knowledge of Him would be possible. The rest of the truth is that "if we love one another, God dwelleth in us, and his love is perfected in us" (I John 4:12). Love is God's life. When we love, we live in Him, and He in us. This "participation" in His life is made possible by His gift of the power to love and by His grace which nurtures and perfects this power in us. It is the sole basis of our knowledge of God while we are still *in via,* but it is sufficient.

Lest this way of putting it seems much too simple, and too good to be true, we need only to remind ourselves of how hard, how "unnatural," it is for us to love as God loves, hence to participate in His life. It is, as Jesus describes it, the strait, narrow, hard way. Yet it is *the* Way. Only by God's grace can we walk in it and grow in it; but as we walk and grow in it God becomes more and more real to us, and we know that we are walking both with Him and toward Him. We know that we are in the light. We know that our final end will be the perfect knowledge and love of Him, which is even now our eternal life and will be our joy forever.

CHAPTER XII

Prayer

IT WAS A SCIENTIST, Dr. Alexis Carrel, rather than a theologian, who wrote the following wise and searching words:

> Prayers, which rise like a great cloud from the surface of
> the earth, differ from each other as much as the personalities
> of those who pray. But they consist of variations upon two
> main themes: distress and love. It is entirely legitimate to
> implore the help of God to obtain what we need. Yet it
> would be absurd to ask for the gratification of a whim or for
> what our own effort would procure. The importunate, obsti-
> nate, aggressive petition is heard. A blind man, seated by the
> wayside, shouted his supplications more and more loudly in
> spite of those who wanted to silence him. "Thy faith hath
> made thee whole," said Jesus, who was passing that way. At
> its loftiest, prayer ceases to be a petition. Man lays bare to the
> Master of all things, that he loves Him, that he thanks Him
> for His gifts, that he is ready to accomplish His Will, what-
> ever it is. Prayer becomes contemplation. An old peasant was
> sitting alone in the back pew of an empty church. "What are
> you waiting for?" he was asked. "I am looking at Him," he
> answered, "and He is looking at me." The value of a tech-
> nique is measured by its results. Every technique of prayer is
> good which draws man nearer to God.[1]

In distinguishing between prayers of distress and prayers of love, Dr. Carrel is making the distinction we drew
in the last chapter between prayers for God's providence

and prayers for God's grace. We offer the former out of distress, the latter out of love.

Like Dr. Carrel, I have no wish to disparage the kind of prayer that comes out of distress and need, prayer for God's providence; but there is need for a balanced diet in prayer. Christian prayer includes five elements: adoration, confession, petition (for ourselves), intercession (for others), and thanksgiving. Confession, petition, and intercession come out of our distress. Yet if they are offered in the mind and spirit—the Name—of Christ, they will express our love. But the other two elements, adoration and thanksgiving, are prayers of love pure and simple; and are not these the elements which most of us most neglect? One of the great spiritual directors tells us that if we have just five minutes for prayer we should spend the first three minutes telling God how we love Him; in other words, in adoration. St. John of the Cross asked one of his penitents, "Wherein does your prayer consist?" She answered, "In considering the Beauty of God, and in rejoicing that He has such Beauty." If we would grow in the knowledge and love of God, we must put first in our prayer life, and keep first, this adoration of God.

Yes; but how? "No man hath seen God at any time." How then can we gaze on His beauty? This is a very real and necessary question. We cannot see God's beauty directly, but we can see it indirectly, as it is mediated to us; we can see it by receiving it and participating in it.

> The mind has a thousand eyes,
>   And the heart but one;
> Yet the light of a whole life dies
>   When love is done.
> —*Francis W. Bourdillon*

Love is the eye of the heart, and through it we can see the King in His beauty. The effort so to see Him is the prayer of adoration, and it is within the capacity of the simplest soul. All that is required is the will, and the effort.

The beauty of God is His goodness and loving-kindness to us, and we see this beauty by realizing it and reflecting upon it. Here is where thanksgiving and adoration link up. The matter, the fuel, for our adoration comes from our thankful remembrance of His mercies past and present. In the early days of my ministry in rural Minnesota I knew a simple Christian man who, whenever he had completed an automobile trip safely, knelt down and offered the General Thanksgiving from the Book of Common Prayer. I remember this so vividly because it is so lamentably rare. Any minister can testify that he receives very many requests for prayers for a safe journey, but very few requests for thanksgivings for safe journeys. This seems to be the critical point at which the ordinary Christian needs to revise his prayer life. Adoration is the highest, purest form of prayer; and it must be fed by thanksgiving.

Let some various witnesses to their joy in God speak to us, that perchance their mood may capture us:

> Serve the Lord with gladness, and come before his presence with a song.—Psalm 100
>
> To breathe is a beatitude.—AMIEL
>
> We need nothing but open eyes, to be ravished like the Cherubins.—TRAHERNE
>
> Gratitude is heaven itself.—WILLIAM BLAKE
>
> We are all strings in the concert of His joy; the spirit from

His mouth strikes the note and tune of our strings.—Jakob Boehme

We bless thee for our creation, preservation, and all the blessings of this life."—Book of Common Prayer

Living as we do in an age intensely preoccupied with psychology we must beware of supposing that this joy in God and in existence has some psychological explanation. There may well be naturally euphoric, optimistic people; but optimism and joy are by no means the same thing. Joy is the portion of those who lift up their hearts unto the Lord in willed adoration and who rejoice in all His works and ways. It is the royal, and direct, road to the knowledge and love of God.

The prayer by which we grow in the knowledge and love of God is adoration fed by gratitude; but this brings us to the inevitable question: How can the heart bowed down by weight of woe adore God? How can one adore the God who seems to have turned His face from him? G. K. Chesterton in his autobiography recalls his maternal grandfather, who was listening one day to his sons as they criticized the General Thanksgiving. Their complaint was that some people have very little reason to be thankful for their creation. The old gentleman broke in to say, "I should thank God for my creation if I knew I was a lost soul!" This is the wisest, soundest attitude. But how do we come by it? It doesn't just happen in us. It must be cultivated, and it can be. It is cultivated by the deliberate, persevering contemplation of God's goodness to us as manifested in "our creation, preservation, and all the blessings of this life." What have we that we have not received? What have we that we have earned, or created for ourselves? What have we that is truly ours? Nothing. Bishop John Higgins of Rhode Island tells of meeting a lady who came into church one day to offer special thanks to God for her baby—who had lived only a few days. She could adore God for the gift which had been taken from her because she had the wisdom to realize that the gift had *not* been taken from her, but that she would possess her child forever in God.

Well established in this lady's mind was the essential point: that we must learn not simply to accept God's will in all things but to rejoice, to revel, in it. But to do this we must somehow transcend our natural childish and selfish possessiveness toward God's gifts. Most of us, in this woman's position, would cry bitterly, "Why did God have to take my child?" *My* child—as if it were in truth so! But we possess nothing, we possess nobody. God possesses all things and all persons. And He, the all-wise who is also the all-loving, knows perfectly what to do with every creature and child of His love.

We find our thought irresistibly leading us into the so-called problem of evil, a subject I should prefer to avoid in this book. But we cannot very well counsel people to adore God at all times and for all things without squarely facing the fact that it is one thing, and easy enough, to adore God when your beautiful child is born, and quite another thing to adore Him when your beautiful child is stricken with leukemia. Our problem lies in the fact that the all-powerful and all-loving God can let this happen. This problem has beset godly minds from the moment when man first saw that God is good, and so long as we insist upon making of it an intellectual problem it will remain with us forever. Our heads demand an answer to the question, a solution to the problem, but our hearts do not. Our hearts ask for a way of living with the pain. The way which God would have us take is perfectly revealed in the incarnate life of His Son. Faced with the necessity of undergoing crucifixion to carry out the Father's will, He wept and sweat blood. This was a scandal even to Him. Yet He adored God, even in Gethsemane. How could He? By what reasoning? St. John records that before His death Jesus prophesied: "I, if I be lifted up from the earth will draw all men unto me" (St. John 12:32). He did not see His crucifixion as being in itself a good thing. It was a monstrously evil thing, done by evil men. Yet God permitted it; and Jesus was content to have it so, for He knew that when God permits the evil thing to happen He intends to make it the instrument of an eternal and glorious good. Jesus had come into the world to draw all men to Himself, hence to God and to life. He had been faithful to the Father, and He knew that through this last and fiercest fight the Father would be faithful to Him. And so God was. After the dying, the rising; and it is from His cross that Christ continues to draw all men to Himself while eternal ages run.

If in our meditation upon the power, wisdom, and love of God we keep coming back to this mystery of joy through pain, victory through defeat, life through death, we find that in our own moments of anguish our adoration flows from a deeper source than in our moments of ecstasy, even though it rises in a minor key. We have not learned to adore God until we can adore Him from a cross of pain.

The philosophers (except the modern ones) have always exhorted us to try to see all things from the viewpoint of eternity. This seems a rather futile counsel. How can we? Only God can see things from an eternal viewpoint. Yet God will share His eternal vision of things with us as we try to see all things with Him, in terms of His ultimate purposes of perfect good. Recall the woman who thanked God for her child who had died. The thinking of her heart must have included several things. She knew that God loved the child infinitely more than she could. She knew that if the child had lived on in this world he might have experienced things worse than death. She knew that God would not allow His child to be cheated out of anything that is worth having. She knew that death could not separate either the child or herself from the love of God. So she thanked and adored God *for being God.*

I may not be able to see things from the eternal point of view; but if I know that God does, and I know God, I can adore Him from out of the darkest depths of woe.

It is primarily, but not only, through the prayer of adoration that we grow in the knowledge and love of God. All prayer, however, will nurture us in this knowledge and love if we offer it rightly. The prayer of confession can express not only our distress of guilt but also our loving desire to be delivered from our sins so that we can love God more and serve Him better. Our prayer of petition for our own needs can express not only our distress of want but also our loving desire for the things we need— health, food, peace, and others—if we are to serve God well. Our intercession for others is an expression of love for those others which is really God's love reaching out to them through us. No kind of prayer needs to be selfish. All prayer can be loving self-donation to God. What will make it so is our loving determination to make it so. We should never pray without first fixing our love upon God; but how can we, if at the moment we simply do not feel any love for God? The answer is that true love for God is not a feeling, and it is not dependent upon any feeling; it is an act of will. The will to love Him is loving Him. No more than this can we provide; no more than this is required of us. We may be sure that as we faithfully persist in willing to love God, He will make it easier for us as we go along by revealing to us more and more of His adorable beauty, by increasing in us that true knowledge and pure love of Him which is our eternal life.

CHAPTER XIII

Worship

THE READER MAY WONDER why separate chapters on prayer and worship are necessary, for are they not fundamentally one thing? A distinction must be made, and it is well stated by Evelyn Underhill, who writes:

> Worship and prayer, though their relation be ever so close, or their overlapping so frequent, must never be treated as equivalents. For worship is essentially disinterested—it "means only God"—but prayer is only in some of its aspects disinterested. One offers, the other asks. "What shall I say, my God, my Holy Joy!" exclaims St. Augustine. There is the voice of worship. "Without thy visitation I cannot live!" says Thomas à Kempis. There is the voice of prayer.[1]

In the same passage Miss Underhill goes on to say:

> "I come to seek God because I need Him," may be an adequate formula for prayer. "I come to adore His splendor, and fling myself and all that I have at His feet," is the only possible formula for worship.[2]

The commonest exposition of the meaning of worship is the analysis of the word itself: worth-ship. We worship that to which we ascribe supreme worth. This is entirely sound, but it is typically Anglo-Saxon understatement or under-definition. "Worth" has come to mean for us little more than moral excellence. We know that man was worshiping God long before he came to believe in the moral perfection of God. In *The Prelude* Wordsworth speaks of

> The rapture of the hallelujah sent
> From all that breathes and is . . .

This is an unintended but superb definition of worship. It is no mere poetic fancy which sees all created things, even stones and grubworms, as worshiping their Creator. Any creature which fulfils its Creator's will for it thereby worships Him.

*   *   *

"God is Spirit; and to worship Him truly His worshipers must offer their worship in spirit and truth" (St. John 4:24, my own translation). These words of Jesus define worship with ultimate authority for Christians. Despite the vagueness in modern speech of the words "spirit" and "truth" there need be no doubt as to what Jesus means. His statement is made in a conversation with a woman who assumes that worship is a matter of doing special holy things in some special holy place. Most of us to this day identify worship with cultic practice. On this reasoning, true worship is correct ritualism. If we are of this mind, we need a corrective word from Ambrose Bierce, who in *The Devil's Dictionary* defines ritualism as "A Dutch Garden of God where He may walk in rectilinear freedom, keeping off the grass."

Jesus Himself participated in the ornate rituals of cultic worship in the Jewish temple, and His word to the woman of Samaria has no direct bearing upon His Church's public worship when it is offered decently and in order. But

He demands a certain spirit behind the acts of worship, and we know what it is: the spirit of loving adoration, full of hunger and thirst for Godlikeness in our own being. To have this mind in us as we worship is to worship God in spirit and in truth.

True worship, then, is the adoring contemplation of God in which there may be mystic rapture but in which there is always something else—the longing to be assimilated in our own being to God's perfect beauty of being. In true worship, as Evelyn Underhill says, we come to adore His splendor, and to fling ourselves and all that we have at His feet.

At this point many a reader may be saying, "This may be true worship, but it isn't for me. I'm not of the mystic sort. I have neither the time, talent, nor disposition for this 'flight of the alone to the Alone' or anything like that." We must face this practical psychological difficulty. Worship is not for the spiritually gifted few; it is for all men. It is made for you, you are made for it. I must make it personal at the risk of being insulting: If there is in you any unhappiness, inadequacy, anxiety, neurosis, or any such flaw, it may well be because you do not worship God in spirit and truth. Your flaw may well result from your excessive self-concern. The only cure for such self-concern is the God-concern, the God-centeredness, which is the fruit of true worship. Such worship is not a luxury beyond your reach. It is a necessity, an inviolable law and condition of your health.

Now some things can be said for your comfort. To be a true worshiper you need have no special spiritual gift. You need not live in a monastery, or in a mountain cave,

or on top of a pillar. You may forget all about hair shirts.
To be a true worshiper you need only to be the person you
are, the person God made you to be.

We turn now to how you can grow in the knowledge
and love of God, the eternal life, through worship.

The doctrine of the Holy Trinity may be one of the
intellectually baffling mysteries of the Christian faith, but
it is not spiritually baffling. Ponder this passage from the
autobiography of Heinrich Heine:

> Ah, my child, while I was yet a little boy, while I yet sat
> upon my mother's knee, I believed in God the Father, who
> rules up there in heaven, good and great; who created the
> beautiful earth, and the beautiful men and women thereon;
> who ordained for sun, moon and stars their courses.
>
> When I got bigger, my child, I comprehended yet a great
> deal more than this, and grew intelligent; and believed on the
> Son also, on the beloved Son, who loved us and revealed love
> to us; and for His reward, as always happens, was crucified
> by the people.
>
> Now, when I am grown up, have read much, have trav-
> elled much, my heart swells within me, and with my whole
> heart I believe on the Holy Ghost. The greatest miracles
> were of His working, and still greater miracles doth He even
> now work. He burst in sunder the oppressor's stronghold,
> and He burst in sunder the bondsman's yoke. He heals old
> death-wounds and renews the ancient right. All mankind are
> one race of noble equals before Him. He chases away the
> evening clouds and the dark cobwebs of the brain, which
> have spoilt love and joy for us, which day and night have
> lowered on us.

This is worshipful thinking about God. Note the child-
like awe, wonder, and tender delight with which Heine
dwells upon each Person of the Blessed Trinity. It hap-

pens that he was a great poet; but could not the simplest rag-picker worship the triune God in the same way? There are no tricks here, and no special skills. All that is needed is a willingness to act upon an impulse which is already deep and strong within us: our natural impulse to worship and adore. All souls have this. The Christian has an enormous advantage in his vision of God in Christ and in his experience of God the Holy Spirit, the Dweller in the Innermost. God is most easily adorable to him who sees Him most clearly and knows Him most deeply. The non-Christian worshiper may hope, or dimly discern, that the awful Power behind phenomena is a Friend behind phenomena. The Christian looks at Jesus and says, "I have seen the Father." Seeing what he sees, he cannot but adore.

Yet this true worship will not inevitably happen in us in spite of ourselves. God leaves to us one necessary thing: to give ourselves over, to surrender ourselves to it.

Christian worship is trinitarian.

To offer it, you begin with the simple and wonderful fact of your creation, your being; and while you are think-ing about your own createdness remember your fellow creatures and the whole creation. It should be easier for us in the space age than it was for our fathers to worship and adore the Father of all, for, behold, He holdeth the infinite spaces in the palm of His hand.

> Deep in unfathomable mines
> With never-failing skill,
> He treasures up his bright designs,
> And works His sovereign will.
>   —WILLIAM COWPER

As you worship the Father your awareness of your creaturely dependence upon Him grows, and this is most healthy and necessary. We are constantly tempted to suppose that we are self-made, and self-making, beings. Thank God, it is He that hath made us, and not we ourselves. This is our holy solace in those moments when we are oppressed by a sense of meaninglessness and futility in our existence. Why are we here? Because the Father and Maker of all has placed us here. We may see no purpose or value in it, but He does; and as we worship Him we grow richly content to be simply creatures whom He had made for His own purposes. Gazing upon the greatness of God we see our own littleness, but we do not resent it or deplore it.

Theodore Roosevelt and his friend William Beebe used to go through a delightful ritual which had in it true worship. After spending an evening of talk together they would go out to do some star-gazing. One of them would recite: "This is the Spiral Galaxy of Andromeda. It is as large as our Milky Way. It is one of a hundred million galaxies. It is 750 light-years away. It consists of 100 billion suns, each larger than our sun." After this recitation, Roosevelt would grin and say, "Now I think we're small enough! Let's go to bed."

Such worship of the Father cuts us down to size; but more than this is needed for our souls' health. Our worship of God the Son builds us up to size—our true, proper size. We are not only creatures, we are sons and daughters of God. As we worship Christ we are given to see our sublime status in God's family and the glorious destiny which he wills for us.

The solid basis of our worship of Christ is meditation upon His incarnate life. Here I would add a suggestion which is firmly grounded in my own experience, but this is a private opinion and no more. It is that the most helpful of the four Gospels for the purpose of aiding and directing our worship of Christ is the Gospel according to St. John. The Christ of the three synoptic Gospels is for most of us more approachable as our brother man. But Christ is the eternal Son of God as well as true and perfect man; He is to be worshiped; and St. John approaches Him, and helps us to approach Him, on bended knee. This Evangelist enables us to see Christ as He now and forever is: the Light of the World, the Living Bread who comes down from heaven, the eternal *I AM*, the Vine in whom we abide as branches, our Resurrection and our Life.

To feed on Christ in our hearts, by faith, with thanksgiving, is to receive directly the knowledge and love of God. It is to receive also a life-giving hunger to be changed in our own being into His glorious likeness.

How can we most fruitfully worship God within us, God the Holy Spirit? On this subject Heine, in the passage we have quoted, is rather vague, but he does make one positive point in saying that "the greatest miracles were of His working, and still greater miracles doth He even now work." Heine had in mind miracles of regeneration, of changed, transformed lives. One of the profoundest of all prayers is found in an ancient Egyptian liturgy of the Eucharist: "We beseech thee, make us living men." We worship and adore the Holy Spirit as God making us truly living men.

In his novel *Jean Christophe*, Romain Rolland notes the fact of continuous change in our inner being:

> As through life we change our bodies, so also do we change our souls: and the metamorphosis does not always take place slowly over many days; there are times of crisis when the whole is suddenly renewed. The adult changes his soul. The old soul that is cast off dies. In those hours of anguish we think that all is at an end. And the whole thing begins again. A life dies. Another life has already come into being.[3]

This unceasing change in us is a most obvious fact; but there is no automatic change for the better. We do not necessarily grow wiser, stronger, more truthful, more loving. Only the working of God the Holy Spirit within us can bring change for the better. But we can adore and worship Him for His unfailing and invincible accomplishment with us. Do we want to become "living men" in the Christ-life, the only true life? Then we have only to give ourselves over to the life-giving Spirit who proceeds from the Father and the Son, and He will make us so.

All Christian worship is summed up in the doxology: "Glory be to the Father, and to the Son, and to the Holy Ghost; as it was in the beginning, is now, and ever shall be, world without end." Worship is the giving of glory to Him who alone is glorious, the Source and Giver of all glory. It is a glorying in Him rather than in ourselves. To this glorying in God we bring our need, our weakness, our failure, our longing to share in His glory by being made Christlike in our own being. His glory is His loving grace. Our glory will be created by the power of His grace.

CHAPTER XIV

Obedience

To be a disciple of Christ is to accept the discipline of Christ; to be subject to Him, to obey Him, to be what St. Paul—the great apostle of liberty—was not ashamed to call himself, "the slave of Jesus Christ" (Philippians 1:1 Goodspeed's *An American Translation*). This slavery is, of course, voluntary; the disciple chooses the yoke of Christ. None the less, the obedience of Christ to which he commits himself is absolute. No Christian manages in practice to obey Christ with a perfect consistency to the end of his days, but he considers his every lapse from obedience a sin.

Because we belong to an age and culture which exalts freedom and generally regards all obedience as servile and degrading, we need to examine Christian obedience very carefully.

The God of the Bible is presented to us under various titles: as our Creator, our King, our Judge, our Owner, our Redeemer, and our Father; but always as the One to whom we are absolutely subject, whom we must obey. When in the fullness of time Christ comes in the flesh, He presents Himself to us as meek and lowly of heart; yet He, no less than the exalted God of Israel, asks our absolute obedience.

Christ's Church, His community of disciples, is sometimes compared to an army. Like all analogies, this one may be used safely if we keep our eyes open to spot the inevitable difference between the two things being compared. In the army, all enlisted men in a given company are under precisely the same orders and are expected to behave in precisely the same way. The philosophy behind this is right—for the army. It does not happen to be our Lord's "philosophy" in dealing with His disciples. The truth is rather that each individual soldier and servant of Jesus Christ is specially created for one special assignment in this world, and if he is to carry out this assignment faithfully and effectively he is to be "reporting for orders" at all times to his Commander.

This is not to deny that all Christians are under the same basic laws. All are commanded to love as Christ loves. All are commanded to pray, to fast, to give alms. Christ did not repeal the Ten Commandments, and He exempts no follower from any of them. There are these indispensable requirements of Christian living which all of us know clearly enough and which are to be obeyed by all. Concerning these we may say that if anyone will set himself faithfully to the hard task of obeying God's laws, for his Lord's dear sake, he will receive one sure reward: growth in the knowledge and love of God. This may be his only reward, but it will be sure—and precious.

Here is a curious fact. Instinctively we resent and resist laws which are clamped upon us by someone in authority. A good but strict schoolmaster imposes stern laws upon his pupils and sternly enforces them. His boys may come to love him, but it will be despite his laws, not because of them. Law usually makes love more difficult. It is not so between Christ and His servants. The more conscientiously they try to obey Him—and the harder they find this—the more they love Him. And we know what makes this difference. The schoolmaster says to his boys, "These are the rules. Obey them, or else!" Jesus says to His servants, "These are the rules. Try to obey them, and I will help you. You have not only my orders; you have my grace to enable you to carry them out." He commands, not as our stern taskmaster but as our loving helper.

We can best see this by looking at a case in point. A thousand years ago, a young nobleman named John Gualbert was looking for the murderer of his only brother. He planned to do the normal, natural thing: a life for a life. On a Good Friday he found his man unarmed and defenseless. The man reminded him of what day it was, and asked to be spared only so that he could devote his life to reparation for his sin. Gualbert answered: "I cannot refuse anything that is asked of me for the sake of Him who died on this day. I not only spare your life, I give you my friendship. Pray for me that God may pardon my sin, and be thou a brother to me in the place of the brother whom I have lost." They joined hearts and hands, and together founded the great monastery of Vallambrosa.

This was an act of pure Christian obedience. We may be sure that Gualbert did it only with painful difficulty. His quite human longing to bathe his sword in the blood of his enemy had to be crucified, and nothing is more painful than such crucifixion of the inner man. It is strongly possible that in that moment his soul rebelled bitterly against Christ for getting in his way. If so, his love for

Christ wavered even as his loyalty to Christ was holding and stiffening; and I suspect that everybody who has tried seriously to be a Christian has known this experience. But Christ gave him a brother. He gave him a work to do that was infinitely more satisfying than the work of revenge. Because in the crisis he obeyed, Gualbert was given the *summum bonum* of life—the knowledge and love of God. Because he loved, he obeyed; and because he obeyed he grew in the knowledge and love of his Master.

It seems to me that Christian theologians generally have failed to see, and to make us see, the true relation between loving God and obeying Him. Milton, for example: his *Paradise Lost* has been one of the most widely and deeply influential forces shaping the popular theology of the English-speaking world. Much of his influence has been biblically sound and thoroughly good, but Milton missed a wonderful opportunity when he dealt with man's duty to obey God. In Book V of his epic he has God sending the angel Raphael to Adam, before the Fall, to admonish Adam to obedience. Why, asks Adam, should man obey God? Raphael answers:

> Son of heaven and earth,
> Attend: That thou art happy, owe to God;
> That thou continuest such, owe to thyself,
> That is, to thy obedience; therein stand.
> This was that caution given thee; be advised.
> God made thee perfect, not immutable;
> And good he made thee, but to persevere
> He left it in thy power, ordained thy will
> By nature free, not over-ruled by Fate
> Inextricable, or strict necessity;
> Our voluntary service he requires,

Not our necessitated, such with him
Finds no acceptance, nor can find, for how
Can hearts, not free, be tried whether they serve
Willing or no, who will but what they choose
By destiny, and can no other choose?

Milton's Raphael speaks for Milton and for most Christian theologians in what he affirms about obedience: that we owe our happiness to God; that to continue in happiness we must continue in obedience; that God gives us moral freedom so that we can choose to obey Him. All this may be true, so far as it goes; but why leave unsaid the most important thing, which is that God wants us to obey Him out of love, so that He can give us the joy of loving Him more? Thomas Aquinas comes close to saying this outright. "The eating of the fruit," he says, "was not prohibited as being in itself evil, but in order that in this small matter men should do something for the sole reason that it was commanded by God." St. Thomas sees such an act of obedience as an act of love on man's part. But even he falls short of speaking the positive truth of the matter, which is that by such acts of loving obedience man grows in the knowledge and love of God, and therefore in joy and life for himself.

It is not worthy of a good God, or even of a good man, to require His children to obey Him as a test of their love for Him. But if the obedience He requires will increase their love for Him and their joy in Him, it is a gift worthy of divinity. This is what we should expect of a God whose name is love. God commanded Gualbert to forgive his enemy, not as a test of Gualbert's love for Him, not simply even out of love for Gualbert's enemy, but so that to an obedient Gualbert He might give more of the joy of knowing and loving God.

*   *   *

All Christians share a common vocation; each Christian has a particular vocation. Our common vocation is to obey the great two-fold commandment to love God with all our heart, soul, mind, and strength, and our neighbor as ourselves. Then, within this common vocation, each has his particular calling, which, like the common one, can be fulfilled only by loving obedience.

But how can one know what his particular vocation is? Anyone who lectures to youth groups especially is constantly meeting this question, and it is usually raised with real anxiety. Behind the question itself generally lies a false assumption that a person's special vocation is something he must look for and find. The truth is that your vocation comes to you; you don't have to go to it. You find your vocation—actually it finds you—in the given facts of your life; and it is God who gives these facts. Among such decisive given facts are those of your sex, the time and place in which you live, your family, your gifts, your assets and liabilities, your opportunities, your relationships. If you are a girl, it is not your vocation to be a priest. If you are an American, it is not your vocation to be King of England.

Your vocation is not your job. At most, your job is a part of your vocation. Your vocation is not primarily to do something; primarily it is to be somebody: specifically, somebody in your particular, unique place in the world who strives in all things to serve and to glorify God. This is your particular vocation, and the will of God for you is to be your rule in the fulfillment of it.

But now we have begged the real question: How can we possibly learn God's specific will for us in any specific situation? Certainly not by opening the Bible with our eyes closed, putting our finger on a text, opening our eyes and reading the answer. The Bible gives us no such directives. Most of us must have "felt for" the late John F. Kennedy when, as President, he had to decide whether this country should resume above-ground nuclear testing, since the Russians had done so. To decide one way would be to risk injury and death to people by fall-out. To decide the other way would be to risk delivering the world into the hands of the communist dictators. Some of us were very happy that we did not have to make that decision personally. Yet, no Christian can evade such necessities of concrete decision in his own life. As a Christian he must be asking constantly, "Lord, what wouldst thou have me to do?"

Here I would repeat something I said about our vocation. We don't have to look for it, we have to receive it. Likewise, we don't have to look for God's will for us, we have to receive it. God's will for us is revealed to us, given to us, *in direct proportion to our devotion and commitment to it.* When we study the lives of the great saints we notice their amazingly sure sense of direction in whatever they do. God's way for them is clear as the noonday sun because their own wills do not get in the way to cloud their vision. Our uncertainty about God's will for us is only the inevitable consequence of our uncommitment to it. So, the only way to get that sure sense of what God wants us to do is to do what the saints have done: to *practice* loving obedience with such consistency and zeal that it becomes habitual. Once we reach the stage where we want nothing except what God wants we shall find that we have the clear vision and the sure sense of direction.

It is in our hearts that we are guided to the knowledge of God's specific will for us, but our minds are most actively involved. We can receive God's guidance only as we both love and think. The word "casuistry" is an ugly word to some Christians, who associate it with the diabolical art of twisting and perverting moral laws to justify our doing whatever we please. Undoubtedly many people have done this; but the right word for it is not casuistry but hypocrisy. Casuistry as Webster's defines it is "the science or doctrine of dealing with cases of conscience and of resolving questions of right and wrong in conduct." Every Christian must be a casuist; there is no escape from this necessity. That is to say, when you have to decide what God wants you to do in any given situation, you must recall God's commandments and then ask: How do I obey Him in this particular matter? Throughout the many years when I was a parish priest living in that quasi-public kind of house known as a rectory, people were constantly showing up at my door to ask my help. God commanded me to help them; this was clear. But how, specifically? If I gave this man with the wife and four children outside in his car the ten dollars in cash which he requested, would he go and buy groceries for his family, according to his word? Or would he head for the nearest tavern? God knew, but I did not, and God did not give me this information as a part of my guidance. If I made a mistake in judgment I could hurt the man rather than help him. What, then, does a Christian in any such dilemma have to work with, as he seeks to know what God would have him to do? He has his intelligence, such as it is, and the ability to use it. He has his experience to date. He has some knowledge of the mind of Christ. Now, there were times, I must confess, when in dealing with the man at the door the dominant desire of my heart was not to do the will of God but to get rid of the man at the door who was bothering me. If, then, I did the wrong thing, it could hardly be said that God failed to guide me aright. But when our dominant desire is the zeal of love, willing only to obey God, and we diligently use all the resources God has given us for making a sound judgment, we shall be guided.

For all of us there are hard cases; but the very hardness of the choices we have to make, as we try to learn and to do God's perfect will in a most imperfect world, has its own way of deepening our love for God by strengthening our dependence upon Him; and with every act of obedience of His will, as we are given to know His will, we grow in knowledge and love of Him.

CHAPTER XV

Devotion

"DEVOTION SIGNIFIES a life given, or devoted, to God." So wrote one of history's most truly devout (devoted) men, William Law, in 1728, at the beginning of his treatise *A Serious Call to a Devout and Holy Life*. Devotion, as Law sees, expounds, and exemplifies it, is *the whole of life offered;* it is not an occasional pious act as is implied by our unfortunate conventional term "devotions" or "devotional acts". Our whole life is given to us so that we can give it—all of it—back to God. So taught William Law. Did he practice what he preached? One day, while still a young man, he was standing at the door of a London shop when a stranger approached him and asked, "Are you, Sir, the Reverend William Law?" On being answered affirmatively the man put an envelope in Law's hands and disappeared into the crowd. It contained a bank note for a thousand pounds. To this day nobody knows who the donor was, or what was his intent; but we know what Law did with the money: he instantly established a school for fourteen poor children. This was purely characteristic of the man. The money placed in his hands was not his, as he saw it, but God's; therefore, to use it in any way other than the way Christ taught him was unthinkable. This is the spirit, the essence, of devotion; which, let us repeat, is the giving over to God what He has given to us, and most essentially the giving over to Him of our own selves to be living instruments and servants of His will.

As we consider devotion as the offering to God of our whole life it may be helpful to recall some words of the late Dom Gregory Dix, who described the Christian life as a striving to "become what you are."[1] We are made Christians by God's adoption of us in Holy Baptism; so from the moment of our baptism through all eternity we are Christians. But our reason and conscience both tell us that it's by no means as simple as this, that we must devote all our days upon this earth to the hard task of "becoming what we are"—Christians. Another great Christian thinker of our age, Karl Barth, declares that "rightly understood, there are no Christians: there is only the eternal opportunity of becoming Christians."[2] If we have made any serious effort at all to be Christians worthy of the name, we know exactly what Dom Gregory and Karl Barth mean. Our Christianity, if we may dare to call it that, can be at best only a striving to "become what we are" rather than a complete achievement, an accomplished fact. I bring this fact about the Christian life into our consideration of devotion because the work of devotion *is* our striving to become what we are in Christ; the life of total self-giving to God is the Christ-life. And we find it most discouragingly, forbiddingly hard. We may recall for our comfort and encouragement that the holiest of saints also found it so.

Jesus lays it down as the law of His kingdom that we "find" our true life only by "losing" it (St. Matthew 10:39, *et passim*). His words frighten the natural man in us, because we instantly think of crosses, swords, pauperism, ostracism, and other such picturesque but daunting terrors. But the "losing" is really a matter of offering, of giving over, our life to One who cares more for it, and has less desire to see it destroyed, than do even we ourselves. When we commit our lives to God in devotion we should understand that not only will He use us, He will care for us, preserve us, fill our lives with blessings unthinkable.

Devotion is essentially a matter of "letting go and letting God." Some sixty years ago, Dean Inge wrote: "All the good things of life have to be first renounced, and then given back to us, before they can be really ours."[3] More recently Dr. Elton Trueblood has put it this way: "A man has made at least a start on discovering the meaning of human life when he plants shade trees under which he knows full well he will never sit."[4] If we agree with these paradoxical judgments, and it is hard to see how any Christian can disagree, we see that devotion, the surrender and offering of our whole selves to God, is the road not to slavery but to freedom. For as long as I consider my money, or my talents, or anything else, as *mine*, mine to control and to dispose of and to do with as I please, the odd and unpleasant fact is that I do *not* own and master that thing; it owns and masters me. At any rate it controls my happiness, my peace of mind, to the extent that if it is taken from me I am miserable. But if, by God's grace, I can so detach myself from my possession that I see it as God's and not my own, to be used by me as He wills rather than as I will, I there and then become owner and master of that which is no longer "mine."

G. K. Chesterton made this observation on things as they actually are with us:

> The man who said, "Blessed is he that expecteth nothing, for he shall not be disappointed," put the eulogy quite inadequately and even falsely. The truth is, "Blessed is he that expecteth nothing, for he shall be gloriously surprised." The man who expects nothing sees redder roses than common men can see, and greener grass, and a more startling sun.[5]

Chesterton was speaking about the "expecting" attitude of the man who selfishly insists that he should get the good things he wants because he earns them. But this false expectancy is simply another aspect of the false possessiveness which so deeply grips us and which must be grappled with and overcome by true devotion at every step of the journey through life. It is the man who sees the roses, the grass, and the sun as God's rather than as his own who sees the redder roses, the greener grass and the more startling suns. So long as the morbid anxiety of possessiveness holds us in thrall we cannot begin to enjoy what is "ours" as God wants us to enjoy it.

Christian writers on this subject have used a variety of terms to designate the action and discipline of the soul which devotion requires: renunciation, self-denial, detachment, sacrifice, to mention but a few. All of these somehow convey the impression that what is offered, given over, to God is necessarily lost to ourselves—as if we can't give something to Him and have it too. But this is entirely erroneous. The truth is paradoxical but indisputable—that we can never fully enjoy a good thing until we have relinquished all claim to ownership of it. Antoine de Saint-Exupéry made a simple observation in one of his books of the truth we are considering here: "There is no savor like that of bread shared between men." What we "devote" to God we henceforth share with God, and in the sharing it acquires a savor it could never have otherwise.

At the beginning of this chapter we recalled William Law's devoting a thousand pounds to God, who received his offering and then moved and guided him at once to set up the school for the poor children. God and William Law took pleasure together in what they together were doing with what Law had devoted. It is always so with whatever is devoted.

Almost all people of reasonable intelligence and some experience of life are well aware of this truth and do not question it—as a truth, a principle. But the best of us strangely resist it in practice. We are victims of what one of the old moralists called the *libido habendi*—the lust for possessing. We have no alternative to striving and fighting against it all our lives. On second thought, we have an alternative: simply to surrender to it. But this is to forfeit life, peace, and the true enjoyment of all that God has given.

Devotion is the offering to God of what we are and what we have. This offering, as an action, takes place in the will. Obviously you cannot physically journey to God and hand yourself over to Him like a fugitive turning himself into the police. Nothing will "change hands" between you and God when you offer. All that needs to be settled in your own mind and understanding is that, henceforth, as the result of your offering, what you have offered is solely God's to do with as He wills. But He will put your gift to work through you, making you a partner in the action and thus a partaker of the satisfaction.

Christian spiritual counselors from St. Paul onward have exhorted us to deny the flesh, and we have too commonly misunderstood them to mean by this a denial of the corporeal needs and pleasures of humanity. But "the flesh," in proper Christian parlance, is not the physical body; it is simply the self, the ego, the natural man apart from grace. This "flesh" is enslaved to the *libido habendi* and is miserable in this bondage. The denial of the flesh, then, is the affirmation of the spirit as the true ruler of life, and the spirit is the will to devotion. When St. Paul reminds us as Christians that we are "not in the flesh, but in the Spirit" (Romans 8:9) he is trying to encourage us in our hard fight and struggle to be devout—to live by offering. He knows that we find it hard. But he would have us bear in mind that if we persevere in denying the flesh and affirming the spirit we shall know the peace of God and the creative joy of God in which we shall share as He accepts our offered lives and works His wonders with us and through us. The flesh is to be denied only so that the flesh may be transfigured, and translated from the shame of self-bondage to the glory of sharing the joy of God as He continues to create and to perfect His creation.

Those who offer most to God love Him most dearly and know Him most clearly, because to them He gives Himself as their portion and their habitual delight.

CHAPTER XVI

Recollectedness

THAT MOST masterful exponent of Christian asceticism, the late Fr. F. P. Harton, defines recollection as "continual, loving attention to God,"[1] and this definition is quite adequate for us. In his exposition of recollection he reminds us of Christ's teaching "that men ought always to pray" (St. Luke 18:1) and of St. Paul's precept to "pray without ceasing" (I Thessalonians 5:17). Our first reaction to such counsel is that it is realistically quite impossible, that no man living in this world as it is can spend all his time in prayer. It could be pointed out that Jesus Himself did not by any means spend all of His time, while in the flesh, in prayer; He spent most of His time, in fact, preaching, teaching, healing, and doing good. So likewise with His servant St. Paul, and with all His saints. But the answer to this difficulty is to be found in the true meaning and nature of prayer. It is a much wider and more comprehensive activity in the Christian life, the offered life, than the word normally connotes. A stanza of a hymn by Whittier is sometimes criticized, as expressing a shallow and sentimental view of prayer. I think the critics are wrong.

> O brother man, fold to thy heart thy brother:
>   Where pity dwells, the peace of God is there;

To worship rightly is to love each other,
Each smile a hymn, each kindly deed a prayer.[2]

It could be reasonably contended that the peace of God, and true worship, and prayer are by no means *limited* to pity, and loving each other, and kindly deeds. Humanitarian though he was, the good gray Quaker poet would have been first to agree. But the truth here is that, within the context of the offered life in Christ, any act of love and kindness done in obedience of Him becomes a prayer.

Recollection, writes Fr. Harton, "is not essentially different from prayer, neither is it prayer diluted; rather it is that practice of the Presence of God (made familiar to us by Brother Lawrence's well-known account of it) which makes every act prayer. It is the endeavour to live one's whole life with God and to do everything for love of Him."[3]

It is an endeavor, an effort, a habit to be cultivated. As such, it involves on our part recalling God as often as we can throughout our day—and night. When you wake up in the middle of the night and find yourself locked in battle with that most exasperatingly elusive foe sleeplessness, you have an opportunity for recollection. It seems to me that such a moment is especially fitted by God's own design for our use in intercession for people in dire pain or distress, whose sleeplessness has some far more agonizing cause than ours. In any case, it is a time for recollectedness of God's goodness and love.

The truly recollected soul, Harton notes, "finds God in all things and all things in God; in those occupations which are miscalled 'secular' it looks beyond the immediate end to the will of God, to which it seeks to relate not only all its doings, but all its desires and thoughts."[4] To any Christian, the job to be done at the moment, be it done in an office or on an assembly line or in a kitchen or anywhere else, should never be just a dull chore. If it is indeed a dull chore, or worse, there's no use pretending that it's something adventurous and thrilling. But if the person who must do it will recall, constantly, that God has given it to him to do, though it remains a dull chore it becomes something much more: a service of the Most High and an advancement of His rule and dominion upon earth, through this dull and lowly work.

It is only through our recollectedness of God Himself, and our place in His loving scheme of things, that we can possibly enter into and enjoy that blessing we so strongly, and so rightly, covet: a sense of the meaning and value of our life as a whole and in all its parts. You can endure virtually any amount of drudgery, boredom, hardship, or worse, all the days of your years if—but only if—God keeps you mindful at every step of the way that it is all for Him, that in you He is well pleased, and that in His good time you shall look upon all this travail of your soul, mind, and body and be satisfied.

Fr. Harton furthermore says:

> Awareness of God brings love, and so recollection is *loving*. The love of God—Charity—is not an emotional thing, and recollection is not an emotional exercise; rather it is an act of the will, the desire for God and the intention to do in all things His most holy will. The man who is in love orientates his whole being and his whole life towards the beloved, so is love the dynamic power of recollection. But the recollected soul is not in a constant state of ecstasy. There may be warmth of affection or there may not—its presence or ab-

sence depends upon the state of the soul, circumstances or the gift of God, and what we may call 'affectivity' is accidental—but the recollected soul is constantly loving God by subordinating its will to His and abandoning itself to Him in actual life."[5]

We cannot hear too often this reminder that "the recollected soul is not in a constant state of ecstasy." It was not until the so-called Romantic Movement in philosophy and art came on to confuse us about love that Christians had any trouble whatever in understanding that love is not always an "ecstasy" of tenderness, or violence, or both. The New Testament and the preromantic Christian writers on the subject of love are quite clear that to love God is to set our will and our minds and hands to the business of doing His will, regardless of whether we feel like it or experience some transport of delight in so doing or not.

At the same time, whatever may kindle our affection and warm our hearts as we do this work of the will— which is loving God—is to be used; for it stands to reason that the more we human creatures enjoy doing anything the better we can do it. Our loving God is subject to this rule. It is a work of the will. But it is often hard work, costly and demanding. If we can enjoy it, we can do it better. To this end it is good to stock our mind and memory with passages of scripture, bits of classic prayer and devotion, and good hymns, especially those which kindle an affectionate and grateful joy in God whenever they are recalled. There are many such. I refuse to make any prescriptions or even suggestions from my own store, because the choice of such mnemonic materials should be strictly one's own. The test of any aid to devotion, be it a verse one recalls or a crucifix one looks at or anything else, is whether it injects joy into the work of loving God, thereby making our obedience easier and our service more rewarding. Jesus teaches us that to be His follower one must take up his cross; He teaches us also that His yoke is easy and His burden is light. There is no contradiction here. The cross in a Christian's life is the denial of self in the service of God. If we love God as we ought, our love does not lighten our burden or lessen our struggle, but fills it with sweetness and joy.

The essence of recollectedness is, as the word implies, the constant recalling of God, remembrance of God, self-reminding of God. William Temple expressed an important and easily neglected truth in these words:

> It is probable that in most of us the spiritual life is impoverished and stunted because we give so little place to gratitude. It is more important to thank God for blessings received than to pray for them beforehand. For that forward-looking prayer, though right as an expression of dependence upon God, is still self-centered in part, at least, of its interest; there is something we hope to gain by our prayer. But the backward-looking act of thanksgiving is quite free from this. In itself it is quite selfless. Thus it is akin to love. All our love to God is in response to His love for us; it never starts on our side. "We love, because He first loved us" (I John 4:19).[6]

Our recalling God's past mercies inevitably helps us to see His present mercies. It is instructive to note that when John Henry Newman wrote his most famous hymn, *Lead, kindly light*, he was evidently in the grip of a deep mental and emotional crisis. He felt a desperate need for some guiding light, but the night around him was dark. But in the closing stanza we see the triumph of a truly Christian recollectedness:

> So long thy power hath blest me, sure it still
>   Will lead me on
> O'er moor and fen, o'er crag and torrent, till
>   The night is gone.[7]

Newman was thirty-two when he wrote those words about how long God's power had blest him on his way. But he had fifty-seven years still ahead of him, with many more dark nights. What he could do, as a Christian pilgrim, was to pause in the midst of any dark passage and recall previous dark passages—and the Kindly Light which had always come and prevailed. In this, he was only a stumbling, groping man, no better than the rest of us. He practised recollectedness, and we can do it as easily and as well as he, if we make it our habit.

Before passing from the subject of recollectedness we should remind ourselves of the part which the Holy Eucharist is meant to play in the Christian's constant practice of the Presence of God. One of the noblest, and least widely known, of Protestant saints was a French-American Quaker, Stephen Grellet (1773-1855). He once testified:

> I very much doubt whether, since the Lord by his grace brought me into the faith of His dear Son, I have ever broken bread or drunk wine, even in the ordinary course of life, without remembrance of, and some devout feeling regarding, the broken body and the blood-shedding of my dear Lord and Savior.[8]

Grellet was a non-sacramental Christian. How much more should the sacramental Christian who lives by the ever renewing grace given in Holy Communion find every common meal a remembrancer of Christ, and of God! Recollectedness is, then, the continuation of the act of Communion as we go about our daily life and work, feeding upon Him in our hearts by faith, with thanksgiving.

CHAPTER XVII

Age

GROWING OLDER, GROWING OLD, can be either a sacrament or a terror. It can be a sacrament of the knowledge and love of God.

Clifton Fadiman wrote these words on his fiftieth birthday:

> At fifty, face to face with physiology, I concede sheepishly that I am mortal. This is the year in which I catch myself turning into a low-level philosopher and reflecting, however ineptly, on first and last things. . . . I rather like being fifty. For one thing I revel in the probability that I will not in the future make very much more of a fool of myself than I already have. At twenty I knew that I would amass the great American fortune. At thirty I knew that I would write the great American novel. At forty I knew I would become a Socrates for sagacity. At fifty I know better. I know I shall end my days semieducated and semisolvent, leaving behind me an untidy trail of forgettable prose. . . . At fifty, one should begin to know what to throw away. To men of fifty I suggest, now is the time to travel light. Carry airplane emotional baggage. . . . At fifty I can afford to look my neighbor firmly in the eye and tell him that baseball bores me; that I think intellectuals are often valuable and useful citizens; that I no longer find any use for more than two suits of clothes; that a household with books in it is almost always more interesting than one with none; that most expensive fountain pens aren't worth the ink they dribble; that I will never write

really well but judge it quite worth-while to spend the next twenty years trying to do so.[1]

Mr. Fadiman reaches this conclusion:

> Now (at fifty) we can begin a new game with a subtler opponent, the person we would like to be. Never quite matching him, we have the pleasure of feeling that at least the struggle is for real and not illusory stakes. To know what we are may well take half a century. To develop that which we now know is well worth the rest of one's life. At thirty, one should measure others, at fifty one's self, at seventy mankind.[2]

In this wise and delightful dissertation upon age, the distinguished critic does not write as a preacher or theologian; but clearly he has absorbed the biblical wisdom about age.

The aging process is a terror to the natural man in us. It is hard to know precisely why, but the explanation seems to lie deep down in our instinctual nature, as a residuum from our original jungle state. Three centuries ago, Thomas Hobbes glumly noted that the life of most men is "solitary, poor, nasty, brutish and short." Undoubtedly it was even more so three hundred centuries ago. When we lived in primitive tribes, we lived for only so long as we could help to keep the tribe alive. If we were men, we could fight and hunt for a while and in this way justify our existence in the tribe. If we were women we were socially useful, hence entitled to live, for so long as we could produce babies—preferably boys. At the age of thirty we were washed up, and there was nothing left but to die, for we had become excess baggage to the tribe. Sometimes the tribe would solve its, and our, problem by dispatching us as one does an old horse. In any case, our years of usefulness, hence our years of life, were few. Thus the aging process became a terror, and has remained so ever since.

The essence of our terror is what it has always been, namely, our fear of losing that which makes us useful or admirable to others. And only one thing can liberate us from this terror. That is the knowledge that our reason for being is not to be useful or admirable to other people, but to be beloved children of God, now and forever. This knowledge of our nature and destiny is given to us through Jesus Christ our Lord. Once we have received it, once it has thoroughly possessed us, the aging process is transformed from a terror into a means of grace whereby each added day brings shining increase in the knowledge and love of God.

Horace Walpole once voiced an odd complaint about life and experience. Life has been badly planned, he said, because experience comes at the wrong end of it; once we have gained it we have little or no time to use it. He compared it to a light on the stern of a ship, which illuminates only what is past—after it is past and it's too late to do anything about it. If the Christian view of man's destiny is right, Walpole was wrong. Our future is never behind us. God leads us through tribulations to patience, and through patience to experience, as a preparation for what is yet to come—the fullness of life and glory.

Seldom do poets sing the possible glories of old age, but Tennyson does so in *Ulysses*. The aged Ulysses is entertaining some old comrades of the Trojan War, and he is not content to live on memories:

Come, my friends,
'Tis not too late to seek a newer world.
Push off, and sitting well in order smite
The sounding furrows; for my purpose holds
To sail beyond the sunset, and the baths
Of all the western stars, until I die.
It may be that the gulfs will wash us down;
It may be we shall touch the Happy Isles,
And see the great Achilles, whom we knew.
Though much is taken, much abides; and though
We are not now that strength which in old days
Moved earth and heaven; that which we are, we are;
One equal temper of heroic hearts,
Made weak by time and fate, but strong in will
To strive, to seek, to find, and not to yield.

The Homeric heroes are not Christian, and Ulysses
dreams of a purely this-worldly glory yet to be won. The
Christian has far better reason to believe that it is never
"too late to seek a better world", since Christians "desire a
better country, that is, an heavenly: wherefore God is not
ashamed to be called their God: for he hath prepared for
them a city" (Hebrews 11:16).

There is no single way by which people arrive at a
conviction of immortality. Some do so by philosophical
reflection upon the imperishable nature of the soul. Some
Christians start with the premise of the resurrection of
Christ, and deduce their own immortality from that. But
something that unfailingly strengthens and deepens the
Christian's conviction of immortality and anticipation of
the "better country" is his life in Christ, his struggle
through the years to outgrow his old self and to grow in
the likeness of Him who is the Way, the Truth, and the
Life. Our conviction of immortality may be very shaky as

we begin our life in Christ; but this conviction takes on bones and sinew with the years if we strive to persevere in Christ's way.

In a small, simple, but extraordinarily weighty book on the life everlasting, Dr. Cyril Alington of England writes:

> Every act of self-surrender increases the life that is in us, and conversely every selfish act diminishes our true vitality. The Japanese, we are told, have a punishment which is entitled, "Death by a thousand cuts": none of the cuts is in itself fatal, but the result is sure. It is hardly fanciful to suggest that a similar result is to be feared from those small, and in themselves trifling, acts of self-assertion and self-pleasing which most of us daily commit. Those who indulge in them are described in the Second Epistle to the Corinthians (4:3) . . . as "those that are perishing," whose thoughts and minds "the God of this world hath blinded." They supply the antithesis to "them that are being saved," who are advancing day by day in that knowledge of God which can only come by self-surrender.[3]

Both our knowledge of God and our blessed hope of everlasting life grow by this daily increase within us of that new life which every act of loving self-surrender to God augments. I venture to call it the process of immortality. As this process goes on in us we become more and more convinced, among other things, that our hard-won experience of earlier years cannot have been for nothing. God let us succeed in some things and fail in some others as a preparation for completeness of life—a completeness which always lies still ahead of us, and will to the end of our earthly life. When William James was seventy, a friend asked him if he believed in immortality. "Never strongly," he answered, "but more strongly as I grow older." When asked why this was so he answered, "Because I'm just getting fit to live." Christ gives to His followers a continuing sense of the present unfitness of their lives, but along with this He gives them a growing sense of their potential fitness for living.

"We glory in tribulations," St. Paul testifies, "knowing that tribulation worketh patience; and patience, experience; and experience hope." (Romans 5:3-4) As the Christian prays, falls, rises again, and stumbles on, the stronger grows his awareness that he is loved with a love mightier than death.

The small child often has a powerful sense of God's love for him, but something usually happens to this as he grows up into maturity. It diminishes or disappears entirely. Some must pass through youth and middle-age, through many years of hard and painful living, with little consoling sense of God's love for them. But if these souls persevere in Christ's way there is given to them in their latter end a dawning vision that all along, through all the weary marches and sieges perilous, God's love for them has been their very life though they knew it not.

I have in my library a "dictionary of last words." Some of these remembered "last words" of dying people are silly, some pathetic, many hysterically fearful. But listen to the last words of some stalwart Christians:

Roger Asham,: "I desire to die and to be with Christ."

Elizabeth Barrett Browning: "Beautiful!"

St. John Chrysostom: "Glory to God for all things."

St. Francis of Assisi: "Welcome, Sister Death!"

General "Stonewall" Jackson: "Let us cross over the river and rest in the shade of the trees."

Henry James, Sr.: "I stick by Almighty God—He alone is, all else is death. Don't call this dying; I'm just entering upon life."[4]

What gave all these their joyous confidence in the face of death was their previous experience of the love of God in Christ. It is a common complaint that nobody can tell us from his own experience what death is, and what lies beyond it, since from that undiscovered country no traveler returns. But such unavailable testimony is unnecessary to him who knows the love of God and has begun, in his weak flesh with its clumsy ways, to love the divine Lover in return.

"Beloved, now are we the sons of God, and it doth not yet appear what we shall be: but we know that, when he shall appear, we shall be like him, for we shall see him as he is" (I John 3:2). When St. John wrote these words he was an old man in Christ, ready to depart. His life in Christ had taught him what was his eternal end: to be made like his Lord in his own being, and to see God face to face. This was not philosophical surmise; this was the direct vision of a Christ-filled heart into the meaning of time, eternity, man, and the love of God. For him this vision grew stronger and clearer as his years increased. So is it with all who share in the common salvation of the King of Love, whose goodness faileth never.

Acknowledgments

Chapter I

1. *The Collected Poetry of W. H. Auden*, Random House, New York, 1945, p. 457.
2. *The Spirit of St. Francois de Sales*, Jean Pierre Camus, trans. C.F. Kelley, Harper & Row, New York, 1952, pp. 1-2.

Chapter III

1. Friedrich von Hügel, *Essays and Addresses on the Philosophy of Religion, First Series*, E. P. Dutton & Co., Inc., New York, p. 99.
2. Pierre Teilhard de Chardin, *The Divine Milieu*, Eng. trans., Harper & Row, p. 58.

Chapter IV

1. Sigmund Freud, *The Future of an Illusion*, Liveright Publishing Co., New York.

Chapter VI

1. John Lothrop Motley, *The Rise of the Dutch Republic*, E. P. Dutton & Co., New York, 1906, II, p. 381.

Chapter VIII

1. From *The Gospel of God* by Anders Nygren. Trans L. J. Trintud. Copyright 1951 by W. L. Jenkins. The Westminister Press. Used by permission.

Chapter IX

1. Walter Nigg, *Great Saints*, Henry Regnery Company, Chicago, p. 26.
2. Albert Schweitzer, *The Quest of the Historical Jesus*, The passage quoted is from the closing paragraph of the English edition. Used by permission of The Macmillan Company, New York.

Chapter XI

1. Oscar Wilde, *De Profundis*, Vintage Books, Random House, Inc., New York.

Chapter XII

1. *Prayer*, by Alexis Carrel, trans. Dulcie de Ste. Croix Wright, Hodder & Stoughton Ltd, London, p. 26.

Chapter XIII

1. Evelyn Underhill, *Worship*, Harper & Row, New York. Used by permission of James Nisbet and Co. Ltd, London.
2. *Ibid.*
3. From *Jean Christophe* by Romain Rolland. Translated by Gilbert Cannan. Copyright 1910, 1938 by Holt, Rinehart and Winston, Inc., New York. Reprinted by permission of Holt, Rinehart and Winston, Inc.

Chapter XV

1. Gregory Dix, *The Shape of the Liturgy*, A. & C. Black Co. Ltd., p. 267.
2. Karl Barth, *The Epistle to the Romans*, Oxford University Press, New York, p. 326.
3. W. R. Inge, *Christian Mysticism*, Methuen & Co. Ltd, London, p. 116.
4. Elton Trueblood, *The Life We Prize*, Harper & Row, New York, 1951, p. 58.
5. G. K. Chesterton, *Heretics*, Dodd Mead & Co., New York, p. 65. Used by permission of The Bodley Head Ltd., London.

Chapter XVI

1. F. P. Harton, *The Elements of the Spiritual Life*, The Seabury Press, New York, p. 274.
2. Hymn 493, in *The Hymnal 1940*. Used by permission of Houghton Mifflin Company, Boston.
3. Harton *op cit.*, p. 274.
4. *Ibid.* p. 275.
5. *Ibid.* p. 275.
6. William Temple, Readings in St. John's Gospel, St. Martin's Press, New York, and Macmillan & Company Ltd, p. 189.
7. Hymn 430, in *The Hymnal 1940*.

8. Quoted by Aldous Huxley in *The Perennial Philosophy*, p. 271

Chapter XVII

1. Clifton Fadiman, *Party of One*, World Publishing Co., Cleveland, Ohio, pp. 15 f.
2. *Ibid.*
3. Cyril Alington, *The Life Everlasting*, The Macmillan Company, New York, p. 68. Used by permission of Basil Blackwell, Publisher, London.
4. *Dictionary of Last Words*, compiled by Edward S. Le Comte, Philosophical Library, New York.